OUT OF THE ORDINARY
NOVALIS **Biographies**

In this series we present people whose life stories, we believe, deserve a wide audience. Here are men and women who lived their lives for others. Here are people for whom the common good was paramount and for whom self-giving was, or became, the most natural thing in the world.

The individuals whose stories make up this series certainly had their faults and failings, but they're nonetheless people worthy of attention and emulation. They are flesh and blood heroes whose faith in God and concern for others make them role models for everyone.

**OUT OF THE ORDINARY**
NOVALIS Biographies

Gem: The Life of Sister Mac
Geraldine MacNamara

A Faith that Challenges
The Life of Jim McSheffrey

Fateful Passages
The Life of Henry Somerville, Catholic Journalist

Travelling Light
The Way and Life of Tony Walsh

# Travelling Light

# Travelling Light

## The Way and Life of Tony Walsh

John Buell

NOVALIS

© 2004 John Buell

Cover design and layout: Caroline Gagnon
Cover photograph: © Karsh/National Archives of Canada/B84680

Business Office:
Novalis
49 Front Street East, 2nd Floor
Toronto, Ontario, Canada
M5E 1B3

Phone: 1-877-702-7773 or (416) 363-3303
Fax: 1-877-702-7775 or (416) 363-9409
E-mail: cservice@novalis.ca
www.novalis.ca

National Library of Canada Cataloguing in Publication Data

Buell, John
    Travelling light : the way and life of Tony Walsh / John Buell.

(Out of the ordinary)
Includes bibliographical references.
ISBN 2-89507-483-6

    1. Walsh, Tony, 1898–1994.  2. Teachers–British Columbia–Biography.
3. Inkameep Indian School–History.  4. Canadian Legion. War Services–History.
5. Benedict Labre House–History.  6. Christian biography–Canada.
7. Philanthropists–Canada–Biography.  8. Catholics– Canada–Biography.
I. Title.  II. Series.

BX4705.W23B83 2004          282'.092          C2004-900726-2

Printed in Canada.

We acknowledge the financial support of the Government of Canada through the Book Publishing Industry Development Program (BPIDP) for our publishing activities.

5      4      3      2      1          08      07      06      05      04

# Contents

# Acknowledgments

This book could not have been written without the assistance, the information, and the material supplied by:

Andrew Baumberg, President of the Board at Labre House; Sr. Audrey Beauvais; Frank Buell; Tony Buell; Phyllis and Bob Burns; Fr. Joe Cameron; John Carley; George Cook; Connie Dodge; Fr. Norman Dodge, S.J.; Dr. Ken Flegel; Katherine French; Sr. Muriel Gallagher; Steve Hagarty; Mary Ellen Holland; Esther Jedynak; Bill Lawlor; Dr. Peter Macklem; Dr. Ken MacKinnon; Jim Martin; Mary McAsey; Fr. Doug McCarthy, S.J.; Neil and Catherine McKenty; Lucien Miller; Patricia Nolan; Dr. Peter and Anne Pare; Steve Sims (and through him, Jamie Godfrey); Lisa Smith; Bonnie Staid, Madonna House, Archivist; Charlotte Tansey; Dr. Andrea Walsh (no relation); Lou Whalen.

## Prologue

I first met Tony Walsh sometime in 1952, possibly in the fall, but exactly when is beyond recall. He stayed so much in the background, and said so little about himself, that he was not a person one "met" with a view to remembering the event, or, years later when he was "someone," being able to say, I met Tony Walsh. He was newly in Montreal, 53 years old, seemingly unaccomplished: he had said little or nothing about his past achievements in British Columbia, and he was quietly talking up a scheme to open a house of hospitality. I was in my mid-twenties, teaching at Loyola College, about to be married to my wife, Audrey. She herself had worked with the poor, through one of the many Sodalities of the period, and with Betty McCabe, whose flat became Tony's first "house." Through friends I knew Steve Hagarty in 1950, and I had known Patricia "Pat" Conners, also in her twenties, since 1947, when we were active in the St. Genesius Players Guild doing radio scripts and dramas, and acting in stage plays. At that time we were to be coached by Jim Shaw, but he was too busy for long script sessions. These people were soon to be, along with Dr. Seng, the so-called co-founders of Labre House.

Life (teaching, graduate studies, domestic matters) kept me from doing little more with these friends than attend the odd meeting and keep up with their news. Pat Conners died in 1953, and much happened to leave Tony Walsh on his own and finally to give shape to Benedict Labre House in its permanent location on Montreal's Young Street. In 1955, after the birth of our daughter, Katherine, I was able to get more involved. Dixie MacMaster asked me to review a book for the Labre House paper, *Unity*, which Leo

MacGillivray of the *Gazette* had just started and was bringing out monthly. Soon I was assisting Leo with the editing and printing and proofreading of the paper, and when a few years later he was too busy to continue, I was able to take on that responsibility.

We held editorial meetings in Dixie MacMaster's room (she was bedridden) once a month, and less often as we became more experienced. The "we" were Dixie, Tony, Marjorie Conners, Murray Ballantyne, at times Fr. Bill Power, and possibly others (we kept no records) as the need arose. We discussed mainly the contents of the next issue. We never had to discuss policy: it was understood that we were not to attack anyone, not engage in debates, not scold our readership. We took it for granted that we were to present "the work," which meant the needs of the poor, the way they had to live, the Christian response, the spiritual life, the intellectual currents of the day, the voluntary poverty of the House. My only promise to Tony was that the paper would come out every month (save for a July– August issue) and on time. In the main we managed to do that. I did it till early 1967, when the pressure of work demanded all my time.

Being on the paper gave me an overall view of the doings at Labre House. To get our news I attended as often as I could the meetings at the House, the Tuesday talks, the Holy Hour, the yearly pilgrimage, the retreat, and tried to meet visitors (there were many). My involvement also meant introducing Tony when he gave talks to Holy Name Societies, sitting on panels discussing what needed to be done in our society, and going to Syracuse to attend conferences organized by Daniel Berrigan's Sodality of professional people. All in all, a chance (some would say a golden opportunity) to gather and keep information for a future day.

But Tony Walsh wanted anonymity and a near invisibility. He probably sensed that with time there would be growing publicity about the House and about him. He wanted none about him. He asked me not to make notes of our conversations, not to keep a file, not to take photos, and not to write about him. I agreed, of course. And with that we could talk freely. It was only years later, in 1983, after he had agreed to let Lucien Miller write about him, that I finally took pictures of him.

The paper *Unity* is a good example of the way Tony did things. He simply let us do our work. He never suggested what the content of the paper should be, never asked us to do articles on particular subjects. He would alert us to news, to coming events, to matters of fact about the House. We understood what he was about, what the "spirit of the House" was, and that formed the basis of a large working group, almost a community. He had to write his column, "Letter from Matt," in busy circumstances, and when it needed some editing, a phone call would settle a doubtful phrase or even a rewrite. He trusted me not to falsify his thought. The House paid the printer. Tony would get letters from readers and would, I suppose, absorb whatever criticism there was. I saw neither bills nor criticism nor letters. I don't think that was a decided policy, it was just the way things were.

I wish now, for the purpose of biography, that I had taken advantage of those years and questioned him thoroughly about himself and his life before Montreal and even before Canada. But once our working relationship was established, I felt I should not intrude on his time. He was very busy with people who really needed his help, and when he was free what he needed was not me, but solitude and rest. Apart from Labre House business and undertakings we had him for supper and a chat whenever he could manage it, yearly, twice yearly, or more often. And true to my promise, I didn't pry into his past.

We named our youngest son after him in 1963, never dreaming that eighteen years later Tony Buell would discover Tony Walsh and be of help to him in his Rielle Street flat. Our Tony did so from

1981 to 1987 when, by then married and the father of a daughter, he left Montreal. It was a fitting continuity. And more than one family experienced it.

Tony Walsh's long and busy life abounds in events and people, almost a century's worth. The present biography is intended to give the general pattern and sweep of his life, and to show the events and undertakings that tellingly reveal the man. Of necessity I have had to pass up a wealth of detail and could only mention in passing the friendships he had with the Berrigans, the Vaniers, and many others, the letters that hundreds of correspondents still have, his travels, the talks he gave, some still preserved on audio tape. As well, I have had to leave out the many Tony Walsh stories his friends have to tell. What is in these pages is at least as factual and accurate as I could make it. May it serve as an adequate introduction to this unusual man.

*John Buell*
*Montreal*
*November 2003*

## From War to Canada (1898–1923)

In January of 1923, a young man by the name of Ernest Joseph Anthony Walsh came to Canada. He came from England, and Ireland in a way, and he had just turned 24 that past December. The dates and his youth are significant. It was some five years after the end of World War I (1918), and he was going to try his luck in Canada, not at home in Great Britain. He had no job to go to, no contacts, no place to start from. He was looking for work, of course, but not to advance a career or to start one. He had no trade or craft, except the informal one of handling horses and the experience of his young manhood. And that, in his late teens, had been of war. All he wanted by way of work was to support himself. So he seemed, to all appearances, to be drifting. He was leaving something behind – in fact, everything – as did many of that "lost generation," and he was entering into a totally unknown future. Just a guy named Walsh, a veteran, like a lot of them.

In the early months of 1923 he would not have been much noticed, and he would have remained unnoticed, had not the rest of his life, the next 71 years, all spent in Canada, made people want to know about his past, and made him finally willing to disclose things about himself.

What is known about his boyhood and youth comes, at this date, exclusively from himself. It comes from the "memoirs" he was prevailed upon to tape and write when he was close to 80; from newsletters he circulated to friends from 1985 to 1993; from information he volunteered to people who knew him over the years; snippets of personal history he may have referred to in conversation, most of which are impossible to round out or verify; a radio interview in 1990; a curriculum vitae for a Canada Council application. Independent documentation is scarce and scanty; no school reports, no family records, none of the now normal bureaucratic paper one accumulates from birth. And independent witness, from those who knew him or his family before he came to Canada, is impossible; it is too late. Today, it is only with the hindsight of his entire life that we can see some of the significance of his early years.

He was born in France, on December 29, 1898, of Irish and English parents and in unusual circumstances. His father, Joseph Walsh, was an expert in horses, a breeder, handler, and trainer, but especially a healer of sick horses, who became well known in Europe. In the late 1880s Joseph Walsh left Dublin, where he could not pursue his growing career and could not go along with his own father's concern for social reform, and went to England where he met and married his English wife, Lucy. From then on, throughout the 1890s, his profession kept him on the move. They were now a family, with a daughter named Anne, and later two boys. In 1890 they were in Hungary, where Joseph Walsh ran a well-known stud farm outside Budapest. From there, as war seemed imminent, they went to Vienna, then to Brussels. It was in Brussels that their two infant sons died. One can imagine what a sorrow that was. Near the end of that decade they were in Paris. But even here the time was turbulent: France and England were at loggerheads and on the verge of war over territorial claims in the Sudan (a matter known as the Fashoda affair). And as Joseph Walsh prepared to take his family to England, his wife went into labour and, in a British hospital in Paris, during a raging gale, gave birth to a boy. At the British Embassy Joseph Walsh had his new son certified as a British subject.

> My father had to give some thought to getting me out of France within thirty days of my birth, for otherwise, as the law was then, I should have had to serve in the French army

when I grew up. My mother's mind was on the baptism of her son. The only location that would do as far as she was concerned was the church of St. Antoine, because Anthony was a saint to whom she had often prayed for intercession during her times of testing, and these were many. A member of the Austrian aristocracy was the godfather, and so I was burdened with the name Ernest Joseph, and Lucy added that of Anthony. My two deceased brothers had been christened by the name of Joseph, possibly for my father, but my own "Joseph" had nothing to do with him.

In January of 1899 the family went back to England.

Joseph Walsh, while a success as a horseman, was also a gambler, though a cautious one, and a spender when he had the money. He was a charming talker in private bars, much admired by the ladies, but always faithful to his wife. In his craft he was something of an artist, in fact a perfectionist. But from the beginning he seems to have regarded his one surviving son as a disappointment. The child was not robust, and his mother was careful not to have this boy succumb to the illnesses that had killed his brothers before him. He could not, and did not, take to the standards of display horsemanship his father sought to impose on him. Joseph Walsh was also a man with a sharp tongue, and this he used in running things and bringing up his son. Its use meant rages and put-downs and sarcasm – never a beating, but always the unrelenting standards of perfectionism. In his rants he'd insist the boy was not his but a changeling, and his rages shook the house like storms. Not an easy man to live with, or to be disciplined by, and the lad got along better with his mother. In all this, someone, probably his mother, had the wisdom to let him have time away from home.

I mention Scotland first although my base would have been really Ireland while our home was in England, because we seem to have spent more time in northern Scotland when I was between the ages of four and eight. It was a country with a countryside and a people that I grew to love very much, a land far different from my home and the associates of my father and mother with whom I would have shared my young life. For me, Scotland meant an opening up to a new and unknown land. For some reason, which I would find hard to explain, my parents gave me the freedom to spend much of the time with the fishermen, gamekeepers, shepherds, and herdsmen…. This was a period of great happiness for me.

It was in Scotland that he first awakened to the beauty of Nature. And from the people of the outdoors, so to call them, "who were illiterate, but were poets at heart," he learned the wisdom of their oral traditions, and from one, old Rob, the history of Scotland. His formal schooling was uneven. In his father's lush times he went to private schools, but in times of less good fortune he went "to whatever little school there might be in the vicinity." Even here, it was outside the curriculum that he found the best things. "One simple school I attended had a fine children's library which had been established by a very unusual sister who was ahead of her time. As both my parents were readers, and I had stepped into their shoes with regards to reading, this sister opened a whole new world to me. She was the teacher who influenced me the most, and it was the books from her library which stimulated my young mind as no other school subject did."

The context of his early life is, certainly, a caring mother, a harsh father, friendly strangers, a love of the outdoors and Nature, and a way of coping: "Such was the life of a small boy completely incompatible with his father, but having a wise mother who knew how to pour oil over troubled waters. In finding my own way, I suppose I discovered the first start of aloneness which is so entirely different from being lonely. I doubt if I was ever really lonely with the hell of loneliness from which most people suffer. Certainly I learned to treasure aloneness because when alone I was free of carping on the part of people who wished to make me toe the line."

Solitude was for reading and Nature, for absorbing the suffering of childhood, for caring for sick creatures (a hobby of his as a boy that was much maligned by his father), for sensing the wisdom of those who worked close to Nature. All that was present as real experience, the mute and inarticulate facts of childhood. It was to remain with him forever. In his early teens, after repeated broken engagements, he finally realized the extent to which he had been rejected by his father. He absorbed that, too, and it, like the rest, remained. Not, it seems, as resentment, but as an openness to understanding others in the same position.

The war, the First World War, changed everything for the Walshes. The great use and consequent slaughter of horses created a need for qualified horsemen to take care of them. "Soon after the outbreak of the 1914–18 war, [Joseph] joined the army. He was stationed at a depot at Woolwich near London. Because of his extraordinary skill in dealing with sick and injured horses, he was in great demand." But it wasn't to last. Late in the following year, 1915, he was wounded, possibly by bomb fragments, and soon died of blood poisoning. The funeral was "in a very depressing Dickens-like barracks," the only mourners the immediate family: wife, daughter, and son. About the funeral, Tony says: "It was one of those foggy, dismal December mornings when I went with my mother and sister to my father's funeral."

The mention of December helps in ascertaining the time. Soon after this, the teenager Anthony Walsh was in the war. "The funeral brought about a consultation with my mother. Although I was only sixteen at the time, I wanted badly to join an Irish regiment. In my eyes my mother was the most unique of mothers, for she gave me her permission. I put a year on my age and through some pull managed to get myself accepted in the army. Before I knew it, I was on my way to the Guards' training depot at Caterham, Surrey." Of his early army days, "I was seventeen at the start of my trench warfare experience, and at that age, no matter how harrowing life might be, it was one of adventure." The fact is he fudged on his age and joined the Irish Guards. He was what we would call now a late teenager, of high school or early college age, a raw, inexperienced kid who had just started to shave. "On arrival at the barracks, Caterham, Kent, I was assigned to a hut of new recruits…. Among the recruits were a number of boys just out of high school…. Because I looked so young, some of the men would remark, 'Say, fellow, you had better go back to school,' or 'Does your mother know that you are here?' The soldiers called me 'Chick' and treated me kindly, for I looked absurdly young, like one newly escaped from the shell."

From the Guards' training depot at Caterham, Surrey, with its typical yelling sergeants, he went to Rawley, Essex, for more of the same, and barracks that were falling down and bad food which led to a strike and to many men being sent off to France in punishment. In these barracks he first met the returning wounded and found that he "could speak to them and get the quiet ones to talk or at least the loquacious ones to talk sensibly." It was a gift, a charism of sorts. It was more than a mere skill or a technique, and he would put it to much use in the future.

What made World War I so bloody was old methods against new weapons. The old methods were men charging across a field of battle with rifles and fixed bayonets until they encountered the enemy. The new weapons were the machine gun and heavy artillery. The artillery devastated a battlefield; the machine gun simply cut down the charging men before they could reach their opponents. Charge and counter-charge. The result: unnecessary deaths in the tens of thousands in a given battle, stalemate, and defensive trench warfare. The solution, late in the war, in 1918, was the tank. And even then the generals stuck to the old ways. Life in the trenches was miserable, dangerous, dirty, and often short. His introduction to the trenches came during the winter months and was worse than he imagined. It was rain, mud to one's knees, duckboards to walk on at the bottom of the trench, pipe tobacco smoke, the tot of rum, carrying sandbags on the slippery duckboards. It was rats, lice, mud and gore. The rats were especially repulsive: "It was for years that I always slept with a covering over my head, because I did not mind the rats going over my body, as long as they did not touch my hands and face."

The final stage of my initiation into life at the battlefront I would not have passed successfully without patrons. Dan and Jess were as different as my father and mother, but as I was a waif at the time, they took me under their wings and became the best of friends and mentors. Together they prepared me for every experience in trench life as though they were training a gladiator.

Dan was a lad from Cork, Ireland, a born leader, a military man, just to all but to slackers a terror. The Lewis gunner of our platoon, he was strong of stature but light on his feet, and at the drop of a hat he would start to box or dance a jig. He had a shock of dark hair and the bluest of blue eyes. Though Jess was an Englishman, he was accepted in our Irish division because he was so genuine a man. He was much taller than Dan, blonde and fair. As in civilian life he had been a gamekeeper, he could read the sky and the earth with precision. He was quiet and calm in crises and did not change with the weather.

Dan trained me for military life. He showed me how to care for the trench, my rifle, my boots. I can still hear him say with an Irish lilt, "Whatever you do, take care of your boots. Remember, now you're in the infantry."

From Jess I learned how to live outdoors simply and, if need be, secretly. He taught me how to care for and pack my clothes, and how to start the cooking fire with special shavings of damp wood so that no smoke would be seen by the enemy. When I finished a job, Jess would always praise me, while Dan would ask me to do something more. They were such opposites yet the closest of friends and they made a wonderful team. Under their tutelage it was not long before I became Dan's second at the Lewis [machine] gun.

He saw battle and bloodiness, and was awarded the Military Medal, which is given for gallantry in action. It suggests a great deal, but details of this event are lacking. The "Memoirs" give short accounts of engagements and close calls, and incidents at the front and the activities of army life on and off the battlefield. And then they come to late summer of 1918.

One calm August evening our battalion assembled in a pasture which was sheltered by woods on either side. When the last commands had been given, the Chaplain rode before each company, giving general absolution. I remember the feeling of being surrounded by magnificent men, bound together in a vast silence, blessing themselves. Within a few hours, many of them would be dead, and many more maimed physically or mentally.

There was a last check of equipment and ammunition. Jess, Dan and I carefully divided the rations among ourselves. The two of them gave me final instructions, and we were off. Before long there came a deafening barrage and men started to fall everywhere. Suddenly above the din I heard my name. Looking back I saw Dan on the ground. Contrary to all rules of advance, I turned back immediately. As I approached him I could see the blood slowly ebbing from his neck. His head twisted sideways, and he was dead.

Life and death were crowded into the hours of that day. The next morning I received news that Jess was wounded. We retired to the back area and were replaced by conscripts. Two days later, Jess was dead. I was numbed by loss....

Possibly for the first time I began to realize the horror of war. Hurt and stranded, I no longer wanted friends. Because I had experience, however, I was called upon to help the newcomers. But though I gave my voice and my hands to them, my heart remained locked. Fortunately after one more serious attack, I knew no more trench warfare. After the deaths of Dan and Jess, my only memory is one of walking vast distances, day after day.

This account was written some 60 years later, with hindsight and a lifetime of experience to inform it. It is Dan's and Jess' eulogy, the pain well hidden, as it were, by the facts in the foreground. But in another, earlier version of those pages he writes: "What had been my heart became like to a stone." That indeed is keening.

It was ineradicable hurt. The shock of knowing his protector was hit and seeing him bleeding the last of his blood – all that in one stark moment. Dan had been the one who gave shape to Tony's young manhood. He was brother, father, teacher, friend, soldier. He showed him what courage was, and bravery, discipline, a sense of justice, and leadership. That man, of all people, was now dead, that way. That man, and then another, Jess, just like him. This is the sort of pain that cannot be assuaged.

The psychology of grieving, with its "permission" to grieve and its promise of "closure," is not there as you experience the horror of the event and the pain of abruptly losing a person. In that loss you lose a world. Gestures of remembrance are empty compared to the sharpness of death and its enforced and absolute absence. Dan and Jess had done something for Tony, given him much, freely, generously, and died in the routine and deadly duty of it. This fact was not lost on Tony, who was then only nineteen.

There was yet another blow to come. As people were celebrating the Armistice, and he too in France, his sister, Annie, who had become a nun with the Sisters of the Good Shepherd, died when the Spanish flu ravaged her community. She was 28.

The army didn't discharge him immediately. He was with the army of occupation at Cologne for a few months, and in England he did guard duty at Buckingham Palace and the Bank of England. He was finally a civilian sometime in 1919.

The war had been a searing experience for Tony. Its effects would take time to wear off. Apart from the war experience itself, and the loss of Dan and Jess, the death of Tony's father had left his mother in difficult financial straits, and combined with Annie's death there was much to grieve over. There was no "normal" to return to.

> Then finally came discharge and release and shortly afterwards the recuperation brought about by spending a year on a large farm of thoroughbred cattle. This was of great value, for after all the excitement there had to be a return to slowing down, an erasing from the mind [all] that I had witnessed. Sleep returned, shattering dreams became less. The work in the fields, the cattle, the exercising of certain animals. I started to stop sleeping with my head under the blankets.... There followed a year at an agricultural college to which I could commute from the small cottage in which my mother was living.

It took him close to two years, from November 1918 to sometime in 1920, to be able to sleep normally and to stop anticipating the nightly rats of the trenches. It is a symbol and a gauge of how deep that trauma went. Fear, however controlled, will out. And that says nothing of the mental shocks that had to run their course, nor of the now totally new situation he was in at the age of 21.

Some 40 years later, in the late 1950s on a bus trip to Syracuse, he referred to that war, and I remember him saying that he never picked up a rifle again. I got the clear impression, implied by his words and the gestures of head and hand, that this was an absolute "No," and that he thought of that war as a great evil. In fact, it would turn out to be the start of the bloodiest century mankind has ever known. Another aspect of this is provided by Dixie MacMaster who remembers him, again in the late 1950s, telling her that, in her words, "he and several friends had thought of joining the priesthood after they got out of the army following Word War I."

A term he used when referring to that war is "reparation." He didn't explain what he meant by it. It comes up again in his "A Statement," his last will and testament, in which he says, "The base of my commitment is thankfulness and reparation...to make amends for the injustice and callousness that people of western worlds caused to primitive peoples." Reparation at its most basic is creating good to replace the evil that has been done. At its most subtle, and on a religious level, that good is sometimes the acceptance of suffering.

One can surmise some such view of reparation on his part. Certainly he never forgot the drama of his young manhood, never forgot Dan and Jess. He wrote of them only later in life, which shows how strong the memory was. It is not too much to say that Tony carried with him a sorrow that could not be cured, like a disease, but could only be assimilated to himself as growth, as spiritual growth. But that is not something one controls, it is something one seeks, and asks for, and receives.

He was a man now, on his own (save for his meagrely pensioned mother), a veteran, ill-treated like the rest of them, looking for work and for a direction to his life. He was hurting, healing, but not embittered. He did not take the route of the "lost generation," the whoring and drinking and the self-pitying posturing of the jazz age. Yet he saw it all, felt it all. In Dublin he saw his friends from the army trapped in a civil war. The sight "of these men begging, or fighting brother against brother, devastated me and drove me into unaccustomed silence." His withdrawal did not go unnoticed, and when his behaviour drew comment and gossip about "poor Lucy's strange son, I knew it was time to leave, and my mother understood."

He applied first to go to Australia, and was refused, then to Canada, and was accepted. He left from Southampton on a ship overcrowded with disillusioned people from Britain and Europe. It was 1923.

## Dedicated Drifter (1923–1932)

From St. John, New Brunswick, his ship's port of entry, young Tony Walsh took a train to Montreal. He would have liked to explore this growing metropolis, but friends he made on board ship had invited him to Winnipeg, Manitoba, where they had a spare room he could use for a few days. That gentle incident suggests a few things: that he made friends easily, that he hadn't planned his destination too closely, and that he wasn't looking for a city job. Canada was vast, and the Canadian West made it look all the vaster, an outdoors beyond imagining. In Winnipeg he soon heard of work at the E.J. Garland ranch in Alberta, and there he went, a hundred miles northeast of Calgary, to Rumsey, near Drumheller. The ranch specialized in Black Angus cattle. Garland was a member of Parliament and usually away in Ottawa with his family, and his foreman ran the place. The day after his arrival, young Walsh met his first Canadian winter: the result was a frostbitten right foot, which led to the amputation of his big toe. It was a wound hard to take for an outdoorsman; it took him a long time to recover from it and to regain normal use of his foot. It also had him look for a home in a warmer climate, which later turned out to be British Columbia.

He spent two years at the Garland ranch, where his experience of the open sky and the flat plains of Alberta, with the colourful variations of weather and season, was "like a balm to a wound." After that he went to Edmonton, where he spent a year doing odd jobs – part-time in a library, a few months laying rail, apprenticing to a carpenter, work on a small mixed farm near Leduc, an area that later became the oil fields. Then, unexpectedly, he had a chance to go further west: a man was needed to look after a carload of pigs bound for the coast. He took the job, and after a semi-comic contretemps riding the freight with the pigs, he reached Vancouver.

It was fascinating country. For a few days he explored, seeing all these new sights: English Bay, Stanley Park, the Second Narrows Bridge, the mountains, especially the Lions, Vancouver's Island (as it was known then), Victoria, the rain forests with their giant trees, Port Alberni busy with lumbering. Then, of necessity, more jobs. He picked strawberries near Mission and polished shoes in Vancouver; he worked on a chicken farm, was assistant cook and did odd jobs at a lumber camp, and got an office job as a clerk, for which he had to learn typing and shorthand. Work was stopped for a while when in a game of grass hockey he was struck hard over the right kidney and sent to hospital and, from there, to recuperate at Kelowna on Okanagan Lake.

Here he met Major Robert Fanning, a fox farmer. Bob Fanning must have seen and sensed something about Tony, because he offered him as job as a partner on his ranch. Two months later, Tony was learning about foxes. It was 1928 and he was turning 30 that December. He would stay a fox farmer till 1930.

On the surface, his was not a very promising life. He would, and probably did, seem strange to most people. Tony Walsh wasn't looking for a wife, or even a career. He was looking only for a job, an outdoor job at that. What he had in mind is not recorded, but it wasn't the usual ambition or desire. He was not given to *machismo* in any way: no beer swilling, no sports buddies, no tavern talk, no yuk-yuk sex jokes, none of the clichés and poses of a phony manliness. He was tough, he'd been there, killer with the killed, and knew what courage was, and grief. No need for fantasy. He had also lived a moral life in the army, not impossible but not that usual, and he lived one now. It was to be remarked on later by the friends he had made. But he himself seems to have said nothing about that. He mentions only Nature and healing. Not a word about his own religious practices. He simply takes them for granted. In notes left by Lucien Miller one reads of a Father Aelred Carlyle, with whom Tony was on retreat in Vancouver in 1930, and again in Princeton in 1932. He was, if not searching, certainly on the lookout for something, but it had not yet come his way.

In 1930, a series of rather normal human events started to happen, their significance apparent only later:

It was in the early fall season when I received a phone call from Father A. Carlyle, a Benedictine monk who was involved in Indian work in the southern part of the Okanagan Valley in 1930....

He said there was a letter in the mail, and when I read it, I was to phone him. The letter arrived and it stated that a teacher had left an Indian Day School at Six Mile Creek, located six miles from the city of Vernon in British Columbia. He thought I was the man for the job.

I immediately picked up the phone and said, "Father, you must be crazy, because I know nothing about education or kids." He remarked that as I was having a week-end coming up, I would be able to visit the reserve.

It was a time of year when all we did to the foxes was to give them apples to bring out the sheen of the pelts. So, I went up and met with the Indian agent, the old chief, and the missionary. They begged me to take on the job, but I explained I would have to consult my partner. He asked me if I wanted to go, and I replied that it was only for six weeks. It could be just another adventure.

So I went. There were thirty pupils. I had been there about a month when the Indian agent came out. He said nothing to me but phoned Ottawa, and they phoned back, and the message finally reached me asking if I would take on the job. As it was near to Christmas, I returned to the ranch to discover that my partner was going to return to the coast where he thought the sea air would give better sheen to the pelts. So I returned to the reserve.

It is clear that Fr. Carlyle knew Tony well enough to steer him to this job. Tony had gotten around in those first seven years. He was in his early thirties now, a man acquainted with Nature, an outdoorsman, a loner, but by any standard upright and quite reliable. He was half Irish and easily taken for British, and this by the British in British Columbia, and by Fr. Carlyle, an English Benedictine, once abbot of the famed converts of Caldey Island, Wales. Who better than this man Walsh to teach Indian children? They – the busy monk, the Indian agent, official Ottawa – were doing him a favour in a way, but it was to be greater than anyone imagined.

Mr. Anthony Walsh, the new teacher, was not only new to Six Mile Creek, he was also new to teaching. Ottawa hired him anyway. It wasn't a very prestigious job. Teaching in general was poorly paid, and a teacher was regarded as someone who couldn't do anything else. Teaching Indians was even lower on the scale. Any white (i.e., non-Indian) teacher would be conscious of that. It was a ready-made preconception. It ran through all of society and at every level. Tony may have been aware of this social distinction, but he had no such preconception. He had several advantages in his favour. First, he was not a teacher, and didn't aspire to be one. And next, he didn't belong to any level or sphere or class of society. He was not a professional, he was not well-off, he was self-educated, he was Irish but he sounded English. He was not a-social, or anti-social, he was just solitary, not part of any milieu. He had been that way since boyhood. He did not see social classes or races, he saw individuals, people, quite apart from their position in society or state of life, from the bums of Labre House to the Governor General of Canada. He described his situation thus:

> As a Day School, the school was located on the Reserve, so the students were able to live at home rather than be absent from their families for the school term as in a Residential School. The school itself and the adjoining house were relatively recently built, and the school room was spacious with plenty of windows. I settled into a simple house consisting of a kitchen, sitting room, and two bedrooms. There was no bath and the toilet was outside.

Since he was not a teacher, in that awful sense, he started off, not with teaching, but with the children in front of him. He was nervous and they were shy, so he began by getting to know the names and faces of some fifteen pupils, seven to fourteen years old. In a few weeks he had seen that "these Indian children were a creative and talented people. They were not dirty and decadent as a certain number of White neighbors thought. Hitherto they had been taught exactly as White children were, in fact, they were almost taught to be White children. Even their Indian names had been carefully kept out of the school room. I discovered that their shyness was a thin mask of protection and that there was poetry and imagination beyond."

One delightful episode reveals both teacher and students in a flash: "Once I tried to illustrate a point by drawing on the blackboard, and they howled with ridicule at my clumsiness. I invited volunteers to come forward to show what they could do. Their originality was startling. 'You see,' I pointed out, 'how much better you can draw than the White man!' From then on I encouraged them to express themselves whenever possible through drawing."

As a result of that rather human approach, the adults slowly came round to see more of this Mr. Walsh, and he to learn more about them. With a doctor sixteen miles away and no resident nurse, he was expected to dispense medicines, which he did, and advise the women on the care of the sick, and, of all things, the feeding of their infants. At one time, when there happened to be no chief, his house became a sort of court where people came with problems for him to sort out. Thus involved, that summer he went to the University of Alberta in Edmonton both to learn about teaching and to find out what he could about the history and culture of the Indians. He sought out Indian spinners, weavers, and leather workers and got assistance from a dedicated art teacher and from people he came to meet from the Okanagan Valley. "For the first time in a long while, I had something really to get my teeth into."

By the end of his second school year, in 1932, his responsibilities outside of school had become too heavy. Since other teachers were willing to teach at Six Mile Creek, but no one wanted to work at Inkameep, south in the same Okanagan Valley, he decided to give it a try.

## Real Art, Real Children (1932–1942)

On a hot September morning, Jim Coleman, the Indian agent for the Okanagans, drove Anthony Walsh, the teacher of two years' experience, and his few belongings south through that picturesque country of mountains, lakes, and rivers, past Kelowna and Penticton to Oliver and there into the Indian Reserve of Inkameep. The reserve was home to about a hundred people, made up of seven or eight extended families. They had large herds of livestock, productive gardens and orchards and hayfields, good salmon fishing, hunting, and berry picking. They also had an excellent leader in their chief. "They should have been a happy people, but they were not. Part of the reason for their depression was possibly the impact of a culture foreign to their own, but I think the main problem was that their white neighbors looked upon them as members of a lower and decadent race." Merely teaching a curriculum would have been easy enough. For a teacher to accept the challenge of the entire situation seemed almost impossible.

Their first stop was at the schoolhouse, which can stand, once its history is realized, as a symbol of everything else. It was green and brown and small.

The only word that could describe the school room itself is "tiny." It had three windows on the west side, five double desks for the pupils, a table and a chair for the teacher, and a pail to fetch drinking water for all. There was also a small wood stove which, I later discovered, gave out good heat during the fall and winter seasons, when the wood was dry. The three blackboards were happily green in color and made the room feel somewhat cooler and more cheerful. Adjoining the schoolroom was the tiniest of kitchens with a little stove, a table, chair and cupboard. The bedroom was equally small with a bed and a simple chest of drawers, and that was all.

Outside, behind the school, were two outhouses above a steep ravine. Light was by coal oil lamps. Obviously there was no electricity and no indoor plumbing.

From there the Indian agent took Mr. Anthony Walsh to meet Chief Baptiste George. (His descendants later used "Baptiste" as a surname.) It is significant that it was Jim Coleman, the agent, who made all these arrangements. The situation, so bureaucratically normal, was full of ironies. Chief George was old now, his hair white and flowing under a Stetson hat, and he had to use a cane. He spoke no English; his son, Narcisse, an only child, translated for him. The chief was highly regarded by Mounties, missionaries, and government, and his reserve thrived as a result of his leadership and vision. But thriving meant meeting the encroachment of the white man. To this end he had his tribe raise herds of fine horses and white-faced cattle for a ready market in Vancouver. Along with that kind of economic independence, he sought a cultural independence as well.

He wanted to ensure that the children of the tribe, especially the eight children of his son, Narcisse, would be able to deal with "the avarice of the White Man." He asked the Indian Department for support for a small school on the reserve, so that the children could be taught in their own context and not in a residential school outside the community for ten months of the year. His request was refused by Ottawa, and he was even criticized by other tribes. So he built his own school, at his own expense, and hired and paid the salary of its first teacher, a black man, the only person willing to work in such a remote area. His action seemed to have shamed the

Indian Department, and after some ten months it took over the running and funding of the school. Tony was its third teacher. It would seem that teachers didn't last very long.

What Chief George wanted to achieve, and Mr. Walsh to start, was to equip the children to live in two worlds, as they would certainly have to, worlds not only different but rival and often opposed. He wanted them to learn English, to deal with the white traders and the stores in town; to understand the business practices connected with raising livestock and farming and selling produce; to retain Indian ways of drying and smoking deer meat and salmon and of dyeing and tanning hides, and also make use of the white man's know-how; to blend their ancient medicinal lore with the new ways and medicines of the whites, who had brought new diseases with them. It was practical, realistic, and wise. But it was only one man's vision, and he was in his declining years. Still, it was a small community, not a vast urban or provincial society, and something could be done.

After they had seen the chief, Jim Coleman brought Tony back to his new home and left. He was alone, in a new solitude. He was later to call it a freedom. The little school building was so hot Tony slept outside that first night, in a sleeping bag under a pine tree, under the stars. He wasn't camping out, on vacation; this was now home, he was on the job.

The schoolroom handled Grades 1 to 8. There were some nine to twelve children who attended class regularly, and sometimes as many as eighteen. Their ages ranged from seven to sixteen, though occasionally one or two were only four years old. Five of these were Narcisse's children; his three older sons had already finished their local schooling. Culturally, and under the circumstances, attendance was not rigid, nor insisted upon, nor restricted. Possibly it was not even mentioned; everyone knew the school was there. Mr. Walsh was more of a live-in tutor than a teacher. But he was still white, and an outsider. What the Indians didn't know was that he also made an excellent guest. As at Six Mile Creek he would have to earn their trust, and this by being true to the children. And Inkameep, too, had the outdoors readily available, with its rivers and lakes, meadows, mountains, and trails, and falls whose leaping salmon delighted the children in the spring. He had spent ten years in those outdoors, the nature of his phrase "Nature heals." Here it was again to surround him, and he to be, now for a third year, with people who understood it and respected its moods and used it to symbolize their spirituality. It would become his other schoolhouse.

It was two years before anything out of the ordinary happened, two years of routine work and, beyond that, of teacher and pupils and adults getting used to one another. And even then what happened seemed totally accidental.

One afternoon some of the younger children took me on a hike in the nearby hills to see pictographs that had withstood countless summer suns and winter blizzards. These striking designs had been made through the application of a dull reddish-brown dye mixed with an oil to resist weather, the same ocher used by the Plains Indians. The pictographs depicted a hunter shooting a deer, a fish, some birds, a few stars, and a sun…. Probably the illustrations went back to the influence of the Plains Indians with whom the Southern Okanagans had had contact for hundreds of years.

Some days later I suggested to the older boys at school that they get their ponies and we ride together over to these hills and make some sketches of the rock paintings. They agreed, and while they were engrossed with their sketching, I took some tracings and photographs myself. Once the photographs were developed, I arranged the most pleasing of the photographic copies along the upper border of the blackboards. The children were strongly drawn to this display of Indian art and began to make corrections of the cruder sketches. Within a few days they started to bring in examples of Okanagan bead work, baskets made from corn husks, moccasins, and even a small drum. From then on different colourful designs made by the children themselves were always on the school room walls.

It is to be noted that it is the young children who took Mr. Walsh to see the paintings, that Mr. Walsh only suggested the older boys make sketches, that it is the children who initiated the corrections, and that they sensed it right to bring in the handiwork they knew so well. All Mr. Walsh did was take a few pictures and put them on display. Simple – simple enough to be unnoticeable. But he had created, in fact he was, a context of acceptance, and he was there to do it. And the children probably knew he'd like the paintings.

This was not art class. It was more like reality. They took it in stride as the good work and normal expression of people, their people, arising from long experience, the experience – necessarily – of Nature and all that went with it by way of beliefs and wisdom. They were, quite naturally, as it were beyond the classroom, discovering and participating in their own heritage. It was what Mr. Walsh had wanted to see happen. It would have been enough for any teacher. But there was more to come.

Again, it was almost by accident, and at the suggestion of Mr. Walsh. They were preparing for their first Christmas concert and decided to use an entire blackboard to illustrate the Nativity. Mr. Walsh suggested, "Suppose that the birth of Jesus had taken place in the Okanagan Valley instead of Palestine. What would have been the setting?" That brought on an outpouring of ideas: not a cave, though there were some in the valley, but a lodge covered with mats made from bulrushes, Mary and Joseph in deerskin, the baby in a carrying board, not an ox or a donkey, but a moose, a deer, and a mountain sheep, and birds, of course, an owl, some chickadees, and a quail. When Mr. Walsh tried to draw these "figures on the blackboard according to their suggestions…peals of laughter erupted behind me." So he asked them to do it. And they did, with great care and revision and concentration. A roomful of artists.

But the surprise was to discover that young Francis Baptiste, who had until then not shown much talent for drawing, had laid out the entire Nativity scene over a major portion of the blackboard. The others had done sketches of the individual objects, but he had done them all. The children were so delighted with what they had done that they begged their teacher to make some Christmas cards of the same subjects. And that they did. They were now doing creative work fully in the traditions of their culture. The subjects were immediate and contemporary, a Christmas season, here at home, blending with more than 1900 years of flexible Christian lore.

Again, the "accidental." Tony sent a few of these Christmas cards to his friends, some of whom wrote to tell him of their appreciation. One friend, Mrs. Dorothea Allison, sent some of the children's drawing to her uncle, Adrian Stokes, a member of the Royal Academy, and his friend Alfred Munnings, the animal painter, who both thought they were very promising. Mrs. Allison then suggested that the Inkameep children should enter the Royal Drawing Society's competition for Commonwealth children which was held annually in London, England. She herself would help the children join the Exhibition through her connections in England.

With Mr. Walsh in the background, Francis Baptiste asked his grandmother, an expert tanner, for a piece of buckskin, and on it he painted his Nativity scene. He did it with painstaking care, watched daily by the children, in the schoolhouse garage where it was stored to await shipment to London. Some ten days before this deadline, one of the children discovered that bush-tailed rats had chewed holes in the painting. Francis Baptiste hurried to get another piece of buckskin and set about redoing his painting, on time. It won the bronze star in the Royal Drawing Society Exhibition of 1936. Apart from the rejoicing and the good (and very new) publicity, this event had two results that Tony had hoped would happen at some time in some way. One was that the older Okanagan people who earlier had been virtually silent about these things now spoke freely about the customs of their ancestors. It was something the young had never heard. The other was more subtle: the whites in the valley were surprised that Indian art had gotten such notice. It was the beginning of a respect of sorts. It would give Mr. Walsh something to work on.

Young Francis Baptiste did a six-panel painting entitled "Indian Boys in Training," showing the rigour of long training in riding bareback, paddling a canoe, spearing salmon, shooting a deer, climbing a cliff, and heaving large rocks – these last to strengthen legs and arms. This painting was later acquired by the Royal Drawing Society, chosen from six thousand entries sent from across the world and the first Canadian painting to be included in the Society's permanent collection. Another of his paintings, "Saint Francis Feeding the Birds," won the Silver Star from the Society in 1937. Young Johnnie Stelkia, also from Inkameep, won two bronze stars. Theirs was genuine talent, and real achievement.

This recognition caused tremendous excitement among the children and from then on, art greatly enhanced the curriculum required by the Department of Indian Affairs. After the regular school day, we had an additional hour for creative activity. Vigorous discussion of art projects developed the children's English. Compositions which had always been unpopular became acceptable when brightened by the addition of pen and ink sketches. Table and health rules were more easily remembered when they were illustrated with birds and animals clad in gay and fantastic human attire. A great deal of enthusiasm was channelled into constructive group projects, as well, especially when the older children volunteered to assist the younger ones in the planning of pictorial compositions.

The children, as a group, now undertook to do a series of six large studies that traced the changes since the arrival of the white man: traders, miners (with camels!), British settlers with their herds, fruit growers, the first paddle steamer on Okanagan Lake, the first train, and present-day life on the reserve. Mr. Walsh

took an exhibit of these paintings and drawings to Europe in 1938 and they were shown in London, Paris, Dublin, and at the Glasgow Fair. The exhibit was seen by artists and teachers of Western art, numbers of whom stated that nothing was being done in their cities that could compare to this art work done by Indian children. They noted that it revealed a keen sense of observation, strength of movement, and subtle humor. The Canadian Junior Red Cross arranged for another exhibit to be shown in some of the capitals of Europe that same year. Again it was highly praised and the children received many letters of appreciation which delighted them.

Tony asked, and convinced, Chief George to let Francis Baptiste go to the Indian Art School in Sante Fe, New Mexico, for a year, so that "he might work with other Indian artists, potters, weavers, and silversmiths." He later became famous as the artist Sis-hu-lk (which means "Moving around").

There was more to be discovered than drawings. Many things in Indian culture had been suppressed by law – tribal activities, potlatch, rituals, dances, masks – and all of it, from the lore and learning of centuries to the very languages, totally discouraged. Again it came from the children, and by "accident." In the schoolroom one day during a period when they were supposed to be sketching at the blackboard, Tony saw one little girl, Irene Baptiste, "put two hands with extended fingers to her forehead and start to walk like a deer making its way furtively through a meadow." Soon the rest of the class had joined in and added other mimes and imitations. Tony knew that the forbidden Indian dances had arisen from a minute observation of the movements of birds and animals. And here they were, fresh as ever, in his tiny schoolroom. Before long he had them creating dances on various themes and making plans to give a program of these to their families. Dances meant music, and music meant drums, and these were found. One rainy afternoon, when all this was still in preparation, and a planned picnic had to be held indoors, another "accident" – little Johnnie Stelkia, who was too shy to speak English often, said he had an Indian story. Tony recalled,

> I was all ears. There was much shush-shushing, for he had broken a taboo. On numerous occasions I tried to coax the children into telling me something of their legends, but they always evaded me. When they wished they could be very skilled in being non-committal and ignorant. Although I had become their friend, I was still a White Man and should not be told Okanagan stories. Furthermore they thought I would laugh at them. The children's general attitude was one result of the repression of government officials who thought it desirable to bring about a complete break with the past.

Little Johnnie told his story in his own language and in his own way: it was about a bear, and Johnnie was transformed by word and graceful gesture and dance into the very action he was presenting. The children soon invented story-dances of their own, and their repertoire began to grow. A little classic was Bertha Baptiste's "Dance of the Four Winds." Bertha was eleven, and they called her Clotilla, which means "Soft Hair."

Drawing, painting, dance, storytelling with mime. There still remained song. And "chance" intervened once again. A friend had sent Mr. Walsh a flashy, colourful poster of an English scene full of flowers, which the children loved, and which, he said, he would put away to give as a prize, in three weeks, for the one who could sing him three Okanagan songs. When the time came, one by one they sang – some sang one on one to Mr. Walsh, too shy to sing in front of the others – and with due praise to all, he announced that seven-year-old Irene Baptiste had won. She had begged and pestered and promised things to her grandmother for the three songs, and when the old lady tired of singing, the little girl had her whistle. Within weeks the class was singing.

To bring all these arts together required something like a pageant or a play. And this could not be left to "chance" or "accident." All this while Tony had made many friends, of course, among the whites, and he had come to know who was doing what in their milieu. Now he turned to Isabel Christie (later McNaughton) who had recreated Indian legends which came to her from an Indian friend, and to Elizabeth Renyi, an Hungarian girl, who had written and acted in presentations at the Oliver Public School. They came up with, respectively, "Why the Ant's Waist Is Small" and "The Chipmunk and the Owl Woman." Tony read the plays to the children, with what dramatic emphasis one can only imagine. The children liked them very much, and with their already acquired skills in drawing and painting, they took readily to costume-making (out of available and cheap materials) and mask-making for the animals in the plays. In June, at the end of that school year, the plays were performed outdoors, for lack of an auditorium or a stage, in a natural setting which served the plays well. The audience was local, of course, and Tony had invited the old people and a few whites. "Something was born anew in the eyes of the Indian elders as they saw the fervor and skill of their children," he said later of the occasion. The whites, who were originally from England and Europe, were touched by the animal legends, the children's acting, and the surroundings, and summed it up by saying, "This is the real Canada."

It didn't stop there. The children started making plays of their own, getting the stories from the old people. They acted them out in the telling, made and accepted criticisms, stayed true to the originals, adding only speeches for minor characters, and let a play take shape while Mr. Walsh took a few notes and arranged entrances and exits. He let the children do the casting by secret ballot. In time, quality increased and a repertoire grew: "How the Turtle Got Its Tail," "The Crickets Must Sing," "Coyote and the Mountains," "The Naming of the Animal People." The group from Inkameep began to give public performances of their dances, songs, and plays. They also had a name for themselves: "Can-Oos-Sez-Skay-Loo," the Animal People.

Mr. Walsh, their teacher, was also busy:

During summers away from Inkameep I would do Indian research at various museums and universities in Canada and the United States – Victoria and Vancouver, B.C., Ottawa, Seattle, Berkeley, New York, and Santa Fe, New Mexico. I learned that the School of Fine Arts at the University of Alberta sponsored summer courses in drama at Banff, and in 1939 I decided to attend. I had heard that the teacher of the drama class, Professor Frederick Koch of the University of North Carolina, was especially interested in folk plays and native art and that creative people from all over Canada and the United States came to study with him. I wanted to see what such people thought about our Okanagan plays and to learn from professionals, and I had hopes that Banff might be a link between our experiments at Inkameep and the outside world. The problem was that I was not an actor myself and had little cash – I think my annual salary was about eight hundred dollars. I could not afford to take along the children. I could bring some of their drawings and paintings, of course, and manuscripts of the plays, but without the little actors and actresses, their masks, mime, dance, and gesture, the mere plays would be next to nothing. As my years at Inkameep had made me intimately familiar with the children's movements and their portrayal of birds and animals, I decided there was no alternative but for me to act myself. It was, I suppose, a preposterous idea, but then my previous nine years in the Okanagan Valley had always been a training in the unexpected.

Solo, he did two little plays, and the quiet power of that chipmunk and that ant touched Professor Koch and his students. Tony got the confirmation he was looking for. The children's art was real and genuine, and his own intuitive sense of it had been right. It gave him the courage to go on.

One of their finest plays and performances was "The Tale of the Nativity," which was done in December of 1939 in a public hall in Oliver, and at night, a first for the children. On this occasion white people from Oliver drove to the reserve to pick up the children and helped them with lighting and setting up the stage. This had a significance of its own. The group performed at a festival in Penticton, and in 1940 at Osoyoos and Oliver. Their busiest time was from 1938 through 1940, and it would have continued had the Second World War not intervened.

Along with these found or natural media, so to call them (speech, song, dance, drawing, and drama), Mr. Walsh "suggested" that a mock radio station might be interesting. The children called it INK, for Inkameep, and they did it with the seriousness of imaginative play. "Every day following the lunch recess, the first ten minutes of class were given to the INK program." At the imitation microphone on Mr. Walsh's desk, the children took turns as MC (today's "anchor"). One result was new talent discovered – a five-year-old boy who could whistle bird songs realistically, a shy girl who could easily manage the program – and, as always, new stories. This radio experience was to stand them in good stead.

In 1941 there came an invitation for the Can-Oos-Sez-Skay-Loo Players and Mr. Walsh to put on plays for the opening in late May of Thunderbird Park near the parliament buildings at Victoria, B.C. They were also invited to CBC Radio in Vancouver to record their Indian songs. This was the children's first trip to the outside world, their first time travelling by train and boat and seeing large crowds. They took the cities in their stride, "but they were awed by the spaciousness of the sea, the wheeling gulls and small fishing boats, and the…little islands with hamlets and farms dotted about them." Their performance was given to a large crowd that pressed the staging area, but the children's voices carried over this, and they mastered the situation. In Vancouver, the CBC radio people expected the group of youngsters to present problems, but INK had done its work and the children performed on cue and without mistakes. Then another performance at St. Anne Academy, followed by a day of sightseeing and feasting, and a train ride to Penticton, during which, in Tony's words, they all "slept the sound sleep of exhaustion."

The little group kept giving presentations and performances and exhibitions until the war and its gas rationing and guarded borders made travel difficult. The work of Mr. Anthony Walsh, teacher, was coming to an end. In his ten years at Inkameep he had done what Chief George had hoped, and more. The Okanagan people on that small reserve had rediscovered and re-expressed their heritage, and could take pride in it. Their white neighbours had learned to respect and value it. Mr. Walsh had helped to set up, with Mr. and Mrs. Albert Millar, the Okanagan Society for the Revival of Indian Arts and Crafts. In 1944, the Society was the first group to submit a comprehensive brief to Ottawa on behalf of Native Canadians. This led to more briefs, by both Indians and whites, and to the reform of the Indian Act in 1949.

One man had started it all, and quietly, with twelve to twenty children in a small school on a small reserve, and he had done it not with protest and demands for social justice, but with arts ancient with every race and new with every child. His many white friends had helped and supported him. But though it was to blossom later, especially in the fame of its artists, it was not to last in the immediate future. Two teachers followed Mr. Walsh, briefly, and a third, calling the artifacts "diabolical," destroyed the masks and costumes the children had made. For a long time even the school remained closed. Today, 60 years later, that period has been rediscovered and researched, in particular by Dr. Andrea Walsh, anthropologist, of the University of Victoria, and the work of Mr. Anthony Walsh is looked at with a sort of mild awe.

In the summer of 1942, while at Banff, realizing that his work at Inkameep had to end sometime, and sensing that this new war would demand something of him, Tony applied to the Canadian Legion War Services. Because of the loss of his toe many years earlier, he could not be a soldier again. But he knew, because he had done it before as a very young man, that he could be of help to the men returning from battle. In November, he was accepted. A final Christmas concert at the school, a last Christmas alone, a farewell gathering, and he reported to the officer in charge in Vancouver on January 2, 1943.

## Another War, Another Start (1943–1949)

He was first posted outside Port Alberni on Vancouver Island at a new army camp built on land that had been forest, its roads still mud, where the Legion had been assigned a hut. It was bare, and his to make "homey." In time and after long delays in getting furnishings, hundreds of men, there to complete their training, came to the now comfortable room to write letters home and break the monotony of their own huts. With the weather often misty and rainy, movies were a near necessity, and Tony, not mechanically gifted, had to cope with broken film and a poor projector. On these occasions, some knowledgeable volunteer would save the day. When another Legion man joined Tony and looked after much of the hut's business, Tony was a little freer to make other contacts.

At the army hospital he met Captain Ed Rosen, a recent graduate of McGill's medical school, who shortly after his arrival had started French classes for the nurses and staff. He was fond of books, art, and theatre, and he and Tony often chatted off hours, 9 p.m. to midnight, in the hospital's kitchen. Ed Rosen got Tony started on basic craft work with the men in the hospital. Through the extension department of the University, Tony was able to organize classical music sessions for the nurses and staff. He never stopped pushing ahead; it became a characteristic of his.

In the meantime, he gathered information about the local Indians. At one of his visits to a residential school, he heard of a man called George Clutesi who was doing some artwork. (The *Canadian Encyclopedia* explains that Clutesi was born in 1905, worked as a longshoreman, suffered a broken back in 1940, and took up his artwork at this time.) Tony met him and liked him and they became friends. And, of course, before long Tony asked him about his Indian background, and George told him of the whale fishing days of his elders, with its attendant risks, and the great ceremonies. He also recounted the legends, beautifully expressed and done with the fine movements of his hands. Tony introduced Ed Rosen to George, and they became friends; George always referred to Ed as "Captain." Tony mentions the two as significant: "the Jewish doctor from Quebec, and an Indian longshoreman and fisherman." He forgot to add the third, the man Walsh, a solitary veteran and one-time teacher. All three were, in a sense, outsiders.

> I arranged that he [George] meet Ira Dilworth of the CBC in Vancouver, and then Lawren Harris of the Group of Seven fame. And George was launched on a part-time career as an artist and lecturer. Then too he got to know Emily Carr who arranged that on her death he would receive her paintbrushes.

Then, typical of army ways, and of the Legion serving the army, Tony was unexpectedly assigned to a camp at Gordon Head, on the coast northeast of Victoria. The camp was called a "conditioning center," a new army enterprise meant to make convalescing men fit to return to fight in Europe. It had asphalt roads, no mud this time, and the War Services hut was in good condition but drab. Few on the army staff, including the Colonel, saw that the men might need more than living in barracks and finding ways of killing time while they regained their health. Tony, on his own, and under some benign suspicion, met the situation by doing things, quietly, slowly, persistently. A simple *fait accompli* avoided hours of indecisive and uncomprehending discussion. He knew what he was about: his two years at Six Mile Creek, the ten years at Inkameep, and his time at Port Alberni had shown him, if not a vocation, then certainly a work that, given the circumstances, only he could do.

At the time, the CBC had a first-rate program called "Citizens' Forum." Radio, which was still a relatively new medium, came into its own during the war, and people tuned in eagerly for any news, censored or not, about the daily progress of that conflict. The program was about Canadian life, and it caught the interest of men who had been in Europe since 1939 and later. Tony formed a group of eight men who listened to the program and discussed it. He acted as chairman just long enough, three sessions, for them to take it over in turn. Before long the less articulate men spoke up, encouraged by their more vocal fellows, and often had the best ideas. From there the thing grew, and from watching these men perform, Tony was often able to guess what sort of creative work a man could be guided to take on.

By one of those "accidents," or coincidences, there arrived in the camp three men with varying backgrounds in art. They were Sergeant Gordon Couling, their leader in a way, a graduate of an Ontario art school; Doug Cameron, an art student; and Austin Taylor, who had trained in Winnipeg. Couling, who was in a cast recovering from a broken vertebra, came to the Legion hut between treatments. He thought the place could do with some paintings, and when Tony told him a little about the small murals at Inkameep, the idea of murals for the hut took shape. The overall theme for these paintings came out of discussions with the men: many had learned from their European experience that Canada's "foreigners" had rich and ancient backgrounds, and they were now seeing their "new Canadians" in a fresh light. The theme for the murals became "Unity."

The work was done, as it were, in public. Sketches were shown in the evening and discussed, with Couling taking notes. As the three artists worked, people dropped in to see their progress: the men, of course, then staff, doctors, nurses, and friends and relatives. Not the best of circumstances for some artists, but slowly the murals got done. Couling's work had a rich variety: a soldier with full equipment returning from war; men and women of the ranks and other services; a group depicting Emily Carr, Anne Marriott, the poet, Bruce Hutchison; and all interspersed with aspects of Canadian enterprise: industry, lumbering, fishing, farming. Cameron's, in broad colours, was about labour, entertainment, sports, Red Cross activities. Taylor's depicted a barrack room scene, a glowing stove, soldiers playing poker; it was popular with the men. The walls of the Legion hut were gradually covered with other paintings and drawings and small weavings, and shelves were put up to display the ceramics the men had made.

Tony also started a mock radio station, which soon became popular and proved to be a help to those men who were trying to recover their full speech. Radio plays, so simple to produce, with few props and nothing to memorize, acquired enough polish to attract audiences. Interest and morale and patient response were so high and obvious, there was no need to point it out. The medical people took notice. Two young psychiatrists came to the camp to see what was going on, and, satisfied that something positive was happening, asked Tony to take on some of their patients. Lack of space and staff allowed only a few at a time. "But before very long, extraordinary things started happening. There was speech recovery, the use of limbs, and also an interest taken in living on the part of a few who had been most morose. None of the men I dealt with had any training in design or crafts, but numbers had come from Eastern Europe who had a background in folk art and crafts. And I never came across one poor design from the hundreds of men who participated in this project." This, it should be recalled, was pre-psychiatric, by an amateur, but one who had learned the human lessons of Inkameep.

When the men decided they wanted an exhibition of their work, they had to convince the Colonel, a new man, of its value, and soon, with Legion support, they started the project. It took a month to make everything ready. Tony asked Lawren Harris and his wife, Bess, to open the exhibit. The officers, who had of course heard of Harris, put on a fine lunch. The next day, a Major-General paid a formal visit and spoke to each of the men. And on the third day, Bernard Webber, Tony's friend from the Okanagan who was now a member of the B.C. Legislative Assembly, came with members of the cabinet and some from the House. The officers' mess honoured them, too. The exhibit had become more than an exhibit. It was starting to have a bearing on ways of teaching, on adult education, on therapy. It reached the public, the authorities, the press. Tony stayed in the background through it all. It had taken on a life of its own.

Tony made many friends like Bernard Webber and Lawren Harris, and many more acquaintances from whom he got information, advice, and assistance, all for the benefit of others, not himself. He was always putting "key people" in touch with each other as a way to get things done. It had become a habit and a way of life with him. It had interesting sidelights: it was through Margaret Clay, the chief librarian at the Victoria Public Library, that he met Emily Carr, whose birds did not twitter and dogs did not bark at Tony's arrival (Carr's test for visitors), and they got on rather well.

The war in Europe ended in May 1945, and men prepared to join the Pacific War. But in August 1945, two atom bombs ended that war, and the city of Victoria, hardly disturbed by the orderly traffic of servicemen, was suddenly flooded with Canadian and British prisoners of war. A hospital ship, a steady run of ambulances to the camp, back and forth, with no let-up, another ship, more ambulances. The prisoners were in a sorry state: exhausted, wounded, ill, most with no teeth, partly blind, gaunt, faces sad, bodies emaciated. Even the tough-guy members of the staff became gentle and caring towards these men. The civilian volunteers, made up largely of women, "did a magnificent job, and as it was years since these released men had seen white women, there were many pathetic scenes, with watery eyes, a lack of speech, and much bewilderment. But after the initial shock was over, then there came a flow of words like to spouting lava."

Tony began putting the returnees in touch with their families and relatives in Eastern Canada. It was a delicate task, and at first he had to cope with the anguish of elderly parents, the hysteria of young wives, some men fainting under the stress, some unable to speak at all. It needed more than an unannounced phone call. With the co-operation of the phone company,

> excellent operators did a first class job in locating families and relatives and then preparing them for my intervention. In a small central room, I would talk to whatever member of the family had been asked for, and I would try to explain the situation of each man and his condition. And then [I would] go on to prepare them for the difficulty of communication, and the great need of their showing a sense of thankfulness, and for them to speak only of the coming meeting, also, just of pleasant things, nothing of tension or hardship – just to try to concentrate on one word, *joy*. And then I would bring in each man separately, make further communication with the party at the other end, and then pass over the phone. Many times I had to support a man who was overcome.

Some relatives, of course, did not follow his advice and gave the men bad news, the worst the desertion of wives.

That work, and all the other work, became too much for one man. Tony organized a small team of caring women to take it over. They did, he claims, a much better job than he was able to do. Eventually, the returnees began going to hospitals in the East, with touching goodbyes. The camp's wartime business was coming to an end.

With that, Tony finally felt the full impact of a back condition that rendered him almost incapable of walking. The doctors tested him and gave him therapy, which brought some relief. The medical officer advised rest and southern sunshine after his discharge. But Tony's obvious success worked against him here. The Colonel wanted him to stay on, and Tony had to convince him otherwise. Tony explained that there were many good teachers available in the coastal area who could take over his work. He then told him of the coming revision of the Indian Act, and explained that with his twelve years' experience with Indian work, he could contribute to the future of the Indians in Canada. The Colonel reluctantly let him go.

He had to recover from his second world war. He stayed with his friends the Webbers, who had four children, which was an indication of how straitened his condition was. "He stayed with us a month after he was discharged from the Legion War Service, when the war ended," Jean Webber said. "That was 1946. We were living at Quathiaski Cove which is just opposite the Campbell River on Vancouver Island." When he was able to travel, he made the long trip south, first by bus to San Francisco, and on to Arizona and New Mexico. In Santa Fe, after some three weeks, he was able to walk with ease. He probably spent a year there, continued studying Indian culture, went to Taos in the winter, and before leaving Santa Fe put on his Indian "show." From there his Indian demonstrations took him to Chicago, then to Penn State College, where the students gave him a lead to CBS-TV in New York. He auditioned his show for CBS, but nothing came of it, and after presenting it at Barnard College, he went north to visit Montreal. There, at this time, he didn't put on his Indian show. Instead, he met someone: Jim Shaw.

Shaw was a journalist (features editor with the British United Press in Montreal), author, literary critic and columnist ("Among Ourselves" in the *Canadian Register* and *The Ensign*), with articles in *Commonweal*, the *Sign* and other magazines. He was one of the founders of the Thomas More Institute for Adult Education in Montreal. He had joined and later left the Jesuits just before ordination. He was widely experienced and knowledgeable, especially about the Catholic world, and very interested in the lay apostolate. He had spent time in New York and knew Dorothy Day. He was a brilliant writer, a man of clear ideas and deep insight, and he was a great help in sorting out the spirituality that went with Labre House. His talent was in his thinking. Putting things into action would be Tony's task.

Some years earlier, in the 1930s, when he was at Inkameep, Tony had received in the mail a copy of Dorothy Day's *Catholic Worker* newpaper. The paper had been launched on May Day of 1933 in New York City, so Tony must have seen a copy sometime after that date. He was impressed by Dorothy Day's work, and especially by her voluntary poverty. It was a fact and an idea he did not forget. Years later, possibly in 1946, certainly before late 1949, he read Jim Shaw's column "Among Ourselves" in *The Ensign*, a Catholic weekly from Montreal. (Mary Branswell, later McAsey, was a young writer and reporter,in the mid 1940s for *The Canadian Register*, a weekly Catholic paper servicing Toronto, Kingston, and Montreal, whose Montreal edition was edited and published by Murray Ballantyne. *The Canadian Register* carried a column by Jim Shaw entitled "Among Ourselves." In 1948 Ballantyne and R. W. Keyserlingk made it into a new weekly, called *The Ensign*, which replaced the *Register* in Montreal, and in it Jim Shaw continued his column. *The Ensign* ceased publication in 1959 or 1960. The term, "The Register" came to refer to *The Catholic Register* of Toronto. Tony Walsh, writing his "Memoirs" in the late 1970s when he was close to 80 years old, may have associated Jim Shaw exclusively with *The Ensign*.) The column was about the lay apostolate, a matter much discussed at the time, and it greatly impressed Tony, who wrote the author to congratulate him. An exchange of letters led to their meeting. In Montreal, Tony had time to see the city. He thought it might be a good place to start a house of hospitality. Jim Shaw seemed to agree.

Tony went back on the road, to Toronto and did his show at the Royal Ontario Museum. B.K. Sandwell saw it and, over lunch, talked Tony into seeing the photographer Yousuf Karsh, who had gotten his start with *Saturday Night*, Sandwell's magazine. From there Tony went to Vernon, B.C., and a job at a fruit-packing company. He kept up with Indian reports and in the spring travelled to Ottawa, where he met with civil servants and presumably gave his presentation on Indian affairs for the revision of the Indian Act. In Montreal he saw Jim Shaw again and they spoke of Tony's plan to open a house of hospitality.

He returned to B.C., made his "headquarters" at Abbotsford, and got a job picking strawberries. Whenever it rained he welcomed the time it gave him to read, "in preparation for the coming departure." (He didn't say what he was reading.)

The die had been cast, and I would have to cut my ties with the West. When I mentioned this to a few close friends, of the possibility of settling in the East, there was consternation, for they were aghast at such an idea and stated with emphasis that I was selling out to the East, that my place was in the West…. From then on I would state when making the rounds that I was going East for an extended period, and these people, knowing something of the ferment of Indian affairs, accepted my statements, but stressed that the stay should be as short as possible.

But Tony Walsh's work in the West was done. It had been for the benefit of others, not himself. From his mid-twenties he followed a barely visible path. It led him to his beloved Indians and to the wounded men of the second world war in 30 years. In his solitary, reflective, disciplined, and moral way of life, he had been able to devote all his time and energy to what he was doing. He had given it all the vigour of his 30s and 40s, and it was to spawn yet more results in the future. But now, that barely visible path had become clearer. It was time to leave.

## A Time of Trials (1949–1954)

Tony arrived in Montreal in December of 1949, a little before Christmas. He was arriving as a stranger, and he was arriving to stay. He was no longer the "teacher," or the "counsellor," or the "social animator," no longer Mr. Anthony Walsh. Nothing of his twenty years of achievement was to speak for him. He was cutting himself off from his standing in the West to become simply Tony Walsh. In Montreal he would be a nobody.

Montreal was Canada's biggest and busiest city, central during the late war, and bustling now on the eve of the 1950s. It was *the* port before the Seaway, *the* rail centre before the 401 and the TransCanada highways, *the* financial centre of the country, rich in manufacturing and in building trains and ships. It was *the* place for "fun" in Canada. It had theatres, and movie houses, and nightclubs, dancehalls, bars, and brothels, and gambling, the very opposite of blue-lawed Toronto.

In this milieu Tony Walsh was just another unemployed middle-aged man. He did little to dispel the idea. To all appearances, he was a bachelor with no responsibilities. It was possible at that time to live that way and attract little attention. The Great Depression of the 1930s and the Second World War had put a lot of men on the road, and socially it was still possible for a grown man to live at his parents' home, never marry, and help to support the family. But Tony Walsh didn't fit that social pattern save in being a bachelor. He wasn't looking for work. He had no home. He had no family – at all, none he founded, none he belonged to, no wife, ever. He was alone. It seemed like folly to come to Montreal.

His one contact was Jim Shaw. And his hope, if not plan, was to open a "house of hospitality." But few understood what that meant. A "house" of that sort could mean a flophouse or a soup kitchen, any place where bums could find food and shelter. But with Tony, as with Dorothy Day, it meant more than that. It meant being poor and living as the poor must live. For Catholics the model, and example, was glaringly unavoidable: it was the way Christ had lived. It was a way he asked some of his followers to live. And to it he added a further startling mystical fact: that what was done to the least of these poor was done to him. This Christ-centred way was inextricably bound with being a Catholic. It was taking God at his word. It was both a pious truism, heard for centuries, and a shock to see it real. It was the shock that would be foremost. Tony had to go slow, had to find people who could understand and support the idea, and then find ways of making the thing practicable.

He rented a very small, warm and cozy room looking on to University Street not far from the Royal Victoria Hospital. He reached Jim Shaw, who visited him and seemed surprised that Tony had come East. Since Jim was leaving the next day to spend Christmas with his mother in New Jersey, he said he'd contact Tony when he got back. But he never did.

On his own Tony scouted the city: Mount Royal with its woods (a mere mound compared to the B.C. mountains), the rivers, the bridges, the churches, the historic buildings now being dwarfed by growing skyscrapers, the old city with its European echoes. He wrote a play about Père Noël Chabanel, the Jesuit martyr (1649) who found life very difficult in North America. It was never produced. In the course of that winter he got to know a few people in Montreal's English Catholic world. Possibly because of, if not directly through, Jim Shaw, he met Murray Ballantyne, editor of *The Ensign*; Dr. Magnus Seng and his wife, Christine, who were involved with the Christian Family Movement; the Karl Sterns; and Dr. John Howlett and his wife, Alphonsine. That summer he held children's classes for the St. Genesius Players Guild. The Guild, founded and run by Fr. Matt Dubee, a dynamic young priest, was well known for its radio and stage productions and its choral group. Tony found this to be a "refreshing undertaking and of course very different from the Inkameep setting."

The following winter he did secretarial work for the Guild and ran Saturday morning classes for the children. It was at this time that he met Fr. Bill Power, chaplain of the Young Christian Workers, and through him heard of Ruth Clevely, who had chosen to live in a poor section of Pointe St. Charles. From Ruth he learned that she and her friend Gertie Keogh were to open a soup kitchen in the fall. He volunteered to help. In the meantime, feeling the need for sun and clean air, he answered a newspaper ad and got a job in the Laurentians, north of Montreal, as a night watchman at a Jewish girls' camp.

The Clevely kitchen opened in September of 1951 at a rented store on Centre Street. The men came, and more men, when word got around that the soup was good. Visitors and volunteers, some of whom would be involved in the yet unknown future, came too. They were Steve Hagarty, newly graduated from St. Mary's University in Halifax and now working in advertising; Patricia (Pat) Conners, in her twenties, an actress and radio dramatist, with a marvellous speaking voice, who had been a pioneer at the Combermere, Ontario, lay community in 1949 with Catherine Doherty, but whose heart condition would not allow her to continue; Isabel Lane, a nurse; and at times Jim Shaw, now living at Cap de la Madeleine and editing the Shrine's well-known Marian magazine. Besides the regular work – cleaning and preparing food in the morning, making meals for staff and volunteers, welcoming visitors for supper – there was, with this sort of people, discussion almost every evening. They were educated, talented, accomplished, eager to live as Christians.

In British Columbia Tony had made a difference in education, in art, in therapy, but in Montreal he was to enter a more delicate area: he was to make a religious difference. He could say later (in the 1980s) of the contrast,

> My kind of spiritual thought remained within myself as I carried on the work of the Inkameep School and the Legion War Service. There were few people that I could actually talk to. When I came East to Labre House the field of work would have been largely Catholic. Then I certainly started to meet some very extraordinary Catholic people. I kind of came into my own, and I had a lot to draw from because of my past experience, which I could relate to whatever the situation was within Labre House. The life I spent at Inkameep with its solitude was a kind of novitiate which enabled me to think through basic things, and it prepared me for the work with outcasts and volunteers in Montreal.

That winter of 1952, when the Karl Sterns took Tony to visit the Foyer de Charité, a place for the severely handicapped that had been started by Cardinal Paul-Émile Léger, a talkative person had kept Tony, who was ill-clad in light clothes, standing for a long time in a biting wind. The result was pneumonia, care at St. Mary's Hospital, slow recovery at the Sterns', then at the Von Rosens' in the country. In the spring he was finally able to return to the city and a life of service.

His room had in the meantime been damaged by fire, and he moved to a new place with the poorest of the poor: three men, one partly blind, one crippled, the other slow of speech and mind, and all extremely kind to Tony. The Centre Street store had run into difficulties and no longer served food, but it was used for other activities. On Thursday nights, Steve and Patricia would come for supper, which Tony cooked on a hot plate, and talk, often in the nearby parks, about bringing out a newspaper that would deal with social problems and the needs of the poor. Pat, whose heart condition made her spend weeks in idleness, had read widely about worship and the liturgy and new developments that had yet to reach most people. This, too, would be part of such a paper. These conversations were preparation for doing something, for bringing something into existence. Tony knew, in a general sense, what he wanted to do and see done, and knew from experience what would work and not work. Better something done than a lot of talk and theory. Still, it had to be learned and tested in the doing.

A critical point was reached when Tony's funds were extremely low, and he started to get by on one meal a day. In short, he was broke and had no food. Decision time. They, that still fluid group, had a meeting: Tony, Pat, Magnus Seng, Jim Shaw – Steve Hagarty was away that weekend. It was October of 1952. Jim Shaw knew of Betty McCabe, a professor of modern languages at Marianopolis College, who had two apartments. The second, for girls in need, was used as a classroom for children in off times. She could no longer afford it, and was looking to sublet. Tony remembers, "Magnus said, 'Ring her up!' Jim did, and she was in and free. So we trooped down to see the place and talked the matter over with Betty. Magnus agreed to pay the first month's rent, and I moved in the second day." The apartment was at 418 LaGauchetière West, south and a little east of downtown Montreal, in an old section of the city. The poor would know where it was.

The following day the first man came, an Austrian who'd been in the Hitler Youth, and before long others, for a meal, for clothing, for a place to sleep. At times the men slept on the floor. But there was no chaos and no voices raised in anger. Soon a routine developed: Tony would go to early Mass at the French Jesuit church, the Gésu. Before breakfast those who wanted to said Prime, a new experience for most Catholics. After breakfast the men went out looking for work or to hospitals for treatment. Lunch was simple and rarely taken by the men. Tony did the shopping, and he prepared the evening meal, ready for 6 p.m. and taken in a leisurely and relaxed way. Later, one of the men, an experienced cook named Tom, looked after the meals, and a friend of his, Ed Charland, asked to stay at the house, and did, off and on, for years. After the cleaning up, Compline was said, also by those who wanted to. Bedtime was 10:30 p.m., rising at 6 a.m.; by breakfast time, the men were expected to be shaved and washed, with their beds made. It was orderly and peaceful, with the basic discipline needed for daily living, and not an organization with structures and rules to conform to. Of the men, no questions were asked, no files opened, no records kept.

"418" was intended to be more than a shelter for down-and-out men. One person (Tony) would live there as his own home, full-time, all the time. Another, Steve, would provide some of his salary for upkeep; another, Dr. Magnus Seng, would guarantee the rent and also run a free clinic for the poor: undernourished children, the elderly fearful of doctors, more fearful of hospitals (where you went to die). The task was not only to heal but to create trust in this underground culture of pain. It was new to have a doctor see patients in their own milieu. Others, Jim and Pat, were to bring out a newsletter. At Jim Shaw's suggestion of "the need of bringing the articulate and trained into relation with the broken," the Tuesday night talks were organized. The speakers were, over time and among others, doctors, lawyers, academics, social workers, wardens, inmates, priests, and of course, Dorothy Day and Catherine Doherty, the "Baroness." The effect was double: the men stayed for the talks and took pride in helping out with refreshments, and the speakers were put in touch, some for the first time, with the real poor. The talks would start on time at 8 p.m. and last for 45 minutes; discussion would end at 10 p.m., often to be continued over coffee in restaurants. With this and the newsletter, which signed itself "the Family at 418," word got round. So did shock.

The shock was that the man who lived at 418 full-time, this Tony Walsh, had accepted total and voluntary poverty. He had put himself at the mercy of others and at the risk of utter destitution. And he had done this as a Christian thing, a sort of calling, if not a vocation, and as a Catholic. And, to make matters worse, he wasn't a priest or a brother; he was a layman, and a non-professional to boot. A house for the poor! What poor? This was Montreal, the city of churches. Didn't the Federation of Catholic Charities look after all that, with the help of social workers and professionals? Here was criticism indeed, and some hostility. It was to be met not by argument but, as with his Indian work, by having people do things and experience the facts themselves.

By April of 1953, the group decided to meet the growing opposition by calling a special meeting, as public as could be managed, on the theme "What 418 stands for." Magnus Seng was to talk of the spiritual aspects of the work, Jim on the apostolate, Steve on the role of the young college graduate, and Tony on the running of the house. But Magnus had an accident when a cab struck him as he was stepping off a curb, and from the hospital he had his notes for his talk sent to Tony, who prevailed on Pat Conners to read them at the meeting. "On the night of the meeting, the place [418, of course] was jammed. I doubt if a cat could have squeezed in, and two-thirds of those present were out for blood. I got Pat to start the proceedings, and so well did she read the wise and compassionate words of Magnus, that the hostilities dissolved like snow under a warm sun. And some of the most adamant critics of that evening were to become our closest friends and most loyal of supporters." The group was hardly a bunch of crackpots: Steve Hagarty was in a glamorous and up-to-date business, advertising; Jim Shaw was a known journalist; Dr. Seng was a noted urologist and surgeon at the Royal Victoria and St. Mary's; Pat Conners had been seen on stage and heard on radio. In that group even Tony Walsh could pass. He put "the work" forward, not himself, and there was no denying that the poor existed.

That crisis, and the now growing relation to the community at large, meant a name had to be found that could readily summarize the house and its work. A deadline was set, three weeks from then, and after much discussion and many suggestions, Tony, having prepared some of the way beforehand, put forward the name of Saint Benedict Joseph Labre. Labre (1748–1783) had been a wanderer, a tramp, a genuine bum, sleeping outside, not being able to wash, going on pilgrimage, always on foot, from shrine to shrine, homeless, penniless, following his solitary vocation. Tony supported his proposal by reading out the lessons and gospel of the saint's April 16 Mass. It was accepted. They shortened it to "Benedict Labre" and the house had a name.

It looked like a success. Magnus Seng's accident would indispose him for a while and other business would make it difficult for him to return, but a young colleague of his, Dr. Ken McKinnon, took over the clinic in Pointe St. Charles. But six weeks after Seng's accident Jim Shaw told Tony he was giving up his editorship at Cap de la Madeleine and going to live on a farm near Farnham in the Eastern Townships (about an hour's drive from Montreal), there to do freelance writing. Of the house, he said, he could write and talk, but he couldn't live there. Unknown at the time, he was and had been suffering from Hodgkin's disease, which gave him incapacitating headaches. It was the reason he left the Jesuits. It goes a long way in explaining his seemingly erratic behaviour, and the drinking which he finally overcame.

Tony understood. And, by a mild coincidence, some six weeks later, Steve Hagarty explained that he was going to enter the Jesuits, and again Tony understood and supported him. Some six weeks after this, now in mid-August 1953, Pat Conners died in her sleep.

With Thomas Merton (1960s). Outside Merton's cabin, known by
his irreverent novices as "Uncle Tom's Cabin." Courtesy of Stephen Hagarty.

Paintings by Francis Baptiste (Sis-hu-lk). Courtesy of the
Osoyoos Museum Society. With thanks to Andrea Walsh.

Paintings by Francis Baptiste (Sis-hu-lk). Courtesy of the Osoyoos Museum Society. With thanks to Andrea Walsh.

Paintings by Francis Baptiste (Sis-hu-lk). Courtesy of the
Osoyoos Museum Society. With thanks to Andrea Walsh.

Paintings by Francis Baptiste (Sis-hu-lk). Courtesy of the
Osoyoos Museum Society. With thanks to Andrea Walsh.

Receiving the Order of Canada from Governor-General Ray Hnatyshyn, Rideau Hall, April 1990. Standing behind Tony Walsh is Dr. Peter Pare. Courtesy of George Cook.

Tony Walsh (left) with Jean Vanier (centre) and Bill Lawlor (right). 1990s. Courtesy of Bill Lawlor.

Tony Walsh with Daniel Berrigan and Anne Pare. Courtesy of Pater Pare.

Tony Walsh, Beauvoir
(near Sherbrooke),
Quebec, July 1983.
Photo by the author.

Notre Dame des Neiges Cemetery,
Montreal, October 2002.
Photo by the author

Fr. Norman Dodge, S.S., blessing Tony's grave.
Courtesy of Steve Sims.

"This great heart had finally given up," Tony said. "And so of the original five, I was the only one left."

It was not what he had thought would happen. He had looked at this undertaking as joining a group, of being a "second Joe," as he put it, staying in the background and supporting the others. Never did he expect to be thrust forward as a leader. His assessment is rather modest. He seems not to have realized that without him none of this would have happened. It was not that he directed events and caused them to happen, though sometimes he did, it was that he had a way of preparing people, and that around him things crystallized and developed. This may indeed have surprised him.

He coped with this new situation, into 1954, and there was yet more to come. A talented con man (who remains nameless in the Memoirs) had talked his way into staying at the house, and did excellent work, which deflected the tell-tale signs of anger and division among the men. There were now eleven people living at the house. This con man organized the men to take on a job painting a house, from attic to cellar, which was to be used as a centre for lay apostolate gatherings. At this time Tony had a chance to go to Madonna House in Combermere for two days with Leo Ramsperger, a friend who was driving to the region. Thinking all was well, he went.

But a few days later, on returning to 418, he found the place empty. Everyone had gone, and stayed gone. The con man had lured all the men to another place. The irony was that Labre House without the poor did not exist, save as a sort of benevolent centre. The poor seemed to have robbed themselves of their very house. And yet it was not really theirs: not theirs to create, not theirs to maintain. Irony had become paradox. Only the mice remained. The everlasting poor.

## The House of Total Poverty (1954–1966)

The pause gave Tony time to think. For a while he was free of house meetings and meals and shopping and the constant cleaning and maintenance. But it turned out to be a period of fatigue and dryness of spirit, so intense he could hardly walk to Mass in the mornings. He said nothing about it, and put on "a good front" to his friends.

> Then by slow degrees it dawned upon me that I had been trying to do things very much on my own and with little thought to the need I had for the support of God. It was a desert experience that I was undergoing…. I was brought to my knees…. Then there broke upon me with startling knowledge that without God's help I was doomed, and my efforts would be worthless. There was only one thing I could do, accept fully, and with the groping full acceptance fear took flight and was never to return…. Though I gained a base of security this did not prevent me from having to contend with suffering and defeat. But always in the background there was the sense of the goodness of God. And this brought about a trust in Him, that no matter how tough the going got, I would come through.

But the challenge he faced remained the same. It wasn't just going the odd day to a place in the poor district and giving food and clothes to those who needed them, and then going home feeling good and perhaps even virtuous. No, it was doing that all day long in some way, and not going home, but staying there, living there, and facing the same thing the next day, and the next, and on and on without an end in sight. It was staying in that poor district, those slums, with all that involved, all the time. It meant not having enough food to eat, let alone to give out, not having enough heat in Montreal's often bitter winter, and not enough cool in the summer, too little clothes, too little money, too little of everything. It meant trying to keep an impossibly dirty place clean. It meant trying to be neat and washed and civilized with other people's cast-offs. It meant being summoned to the door anytime, all the time, by those whose needs precluded politeness and gratitude. It meant being taken for a madman for wanting to be there at all – both from the well-off who dreaded the slums and those who were the slums. And all these facts and factors, one upon the other, often all at once, formed a constant and continuing condition, relieved only by what appeared to be the random donations of strangers. Nothing glamorous here, no applause, or publicity, which he shunned, and no redeeming features at all, save himself, which could be of no benefit to him. It seemed permanent, unchanging, drab, as ineradicable as the smell of poverty. And yet he stayed. He stayed by choice, voluntarily, which was different from being poor by hard circumstance, and involuntarily, and often bitterly.

What kept him to that grind of organized routine and activity, often hectic no matter how well planned, was more than a sense of social injustice, or a desire to set things right. It was an interiority that relied on daily Mass, on times of withdrawal and quiet, if he could find them, and on habits of thought and prayer formed in solitude over the years. Of these he never spoke, never offered them as a "program" for others to follow. They are evident from what he did, from what was there to be seen externally: the Mass, Benediction, a silent holy hour before the Blessed Sacrament, his keeping to Prime and Compline, his love of nature and its creator, the solitary reading and letter-writing or just musing in the country where he visited friends, which made him an easy guest. And always, back to work.

Other, new men would turn up, of course. He had the experience now to run an even better house. And there had been developments. Marjorie Conners, Pat's mother, a psychiatric nurse, decided at the age of 64 to open a house for women, and to do it fully by living there in voluntary poverty. It was to be called Patricia House. The house was at 207 Murray Street in that general slum area, an old two-storey wooden house, off plumb, the first floor of which was Marjorie's, the second that of the Little Sisters of Jesus (inspired by Charles de Foucauld), who had arrived from France about the time 418 was started. Later, at the Little Sisters' chapel on Thursday evenings, the Labre House people would hold an hour of silent adoration. Patricia House was meant to open on the anniversary of Pat's death (18 August), but with needed repairs it opened in November 1954.

Another key person was Dixie MacMaster, whom Jim Shaw had taken Tony to see sometime in 1951. She was another paradox. She was a shut-in, bedridden, with most of her bones fused and rigid, and she had been that way since 1930 when at fifteen she was struck with severe rheumatoid arthritis. She could move her gnarled hands with difficulty, her head within a narrow angle, and sit propped up in bed, and with a delicate back-scratcher she could maneuver things on a bed tray. At 24 she had discovered the spiritual world of her Catholicism. From London she acquired one, then a second, then (with difficulty because of the war) the other two of the four volumes of the English breviary. She had read widely on the liturgy and worship, and this, Tony always insisted, was a dimension Labre House must have. They invited her to be the sixth so-called founding member, and she remained in the middle of things: editorial meetings in her room, visits, drop-ins from out of town, like Dorothy Day and Bob Lax, the minimalist poet and close friend of Thomas Merton. She wrote articles and book reviews (typed by volunteers) and got others to write, and later in Antigonish, where her family retired, she was at the heart of a group that started a l'Arche community. Among others who visited Dixie were Malcolm Muggeridge, Mother Teresa and Jean Vanier.

Leo MacGillivray, city editor of the *Gazette*, Montreal's morning paper, took on the task of making the newsletter into a small newspaper. It had to be poor, but only in cost, not in talent or quality. He found a French print shop off-island, some 30 miles southwest of the city near Châteauguay. The paper was to be a monthly four-page tabloid. At a meeting held at Dixie's, Murray Ballantyne suggested the name *Unity*. Leo quietly insisted on news and facts, rather than relying on "timeless think-pieces," of which there was always a steady supply. The first issue came out in April 1955. Leo's professionalism was continued as a policy by those who had in effect been trained by him. He was too modest ever to claim credit. The paper never attacked anybody, never denounced, never engaged in argument. It presented facts, often street facts, the poor and their conditions, news of what people were doing, and of course the thinking all this involved. The core of the paper was always "The Daily Round," which was Tony's diary of events; Marjorie Conners' "Patricia House," her anecdotal accounts of the lives of the poor, always well written; and "Letter from Matt," Tony's pseudonymous thoughts sent to various fictional (in name only) friends. From a journalistic angle, this looked repetitious, but today it offers a rare look at the on-the-spot history of the House.

Another person whose help was crucial was Murray Ballantyne. He presents a paradox of a different kind: a wealthy man in this enterprise of poverty. A convert from 1933, he brought out *The Montreal Beacon* (1938), *The Canadian Register*, and *The Ensign*, from which he withdrew in 1949 when, in the Duplessis era, Archbishop Charbonneau was forced to leave office. He volunteered his resources and assistance in resettling displaced persons (DPs) after the Second World War. He hired Jim Shaw as a writer, and introduced him to Dr. Magnus Seng as "a man who needed a family." It was through Murray's friend Yvonne Lyon that Tony met Pauline Vanier, newly returned from France where her husband, Georges Vanier, had been ambassador from 1944 to 1953. Yvonne Lyon, who by then was elderly, and had been among the first to organize the Sunday dinners at Labre House, introduced Madame Vanier to the house, and Pauline was a frequent visitor and worker. She often had the men at the table laughing, a rare occurrence. The story that she scrubbed floors on her hands and knees is legend.

What is not legend is that when Madame Vanier, during Georges Vanier's term as Governor-General of Canada (1959–1967), invited Tony to Government House, she asked him to borrow a black suit and a white shirt and black tie, and not to come to Government House "with your pajamas and toothbrush in a paper bag." She knew her Tony. The occasion was, however, serious. She wanted Tony to talk with Dr. Wilder Penfield about her son Jean. The Vaniers were getting criticism and pressure about their "Jock" (so named as an infant by his Scottish nurse). Jean had recently completed his doctorate in philosophy and was resigning his commission with the Canadian Navy. His plan, which he carried out in 1964, was to get a house in Trosly-Breuil, near Paris, and care for two mentally handicapped men. Tony had earlier reassured the Vaniers of the soundness of Jean's decision, now reflected in L'Arche and its houses worldwide. During that famous weekend at Government House, Tony was twice invited for a chat with Dr. Penfield, who was very interested, if not totally convinced. Little did Murray Ballantyne know what having tea with the elderly and tiny Yvonne Lyon would lead to for Tony.

Murray kept his role at Labre House as hidden and anonymous as possible, and he helped it through many a financial crisis. It was he who enabled Labre House and Patricia House to own their own buildings. He had said of Tony's crisis at 418 when he found himself alone, "We couldn't let him starve." Catherine Doherty, the "B," called Murray "the wealthy man who was poor."

Homeless men kept coming. New help came, too, and new problems: 418 LaGauchetière had too many people living there, a violation of the city's fire regulations. In January 1955, the House had to move to a new location – 123 Duke Street in Griffintown, some six blocks south and west of 418. By the end of that year it moved to 122 Duke Street for a few weeks, and finally, in 1956, a few blocks further west to 308 Young Street, a three-storey row house. The man who bought it, the anonymous Murray Ballantyne, let them have it rent-free on condition that they keep it in good repair and pay the taxes. In 1961, when he had to sell it, members and friends thought it best to buy it – for $8,000, the original price, to be paid in one or many sums, without interest. A fund drive paid it off in a year. To do all this, they incorporated themselves. That way Tony still didn't own anything.

Tony insisted on staying small. He often refused large sums of money and the practical schemes to make the place more efficient. If the work grew too much for one house, the answer was to open another house, in turn to remain small. He seemed to take it for granted that someone would take to voluntary poverty. With hindsight one can see that his was a special vocation.

Events proved him right about being small. His now lifelong habit of finding key people, putting them in touch with one another, and quietly pointing out needs and ways of meeting them began to get its usual results. Without referring to his own role, Tony says of this beginning,

> There then started the giving out of Sunday meals. These meals were given to older men living in small rooms, but who also came for clothes and the occasional meal. The first of these meals were prepared and served by Phonsine [Howlett] and Betty Mennie. Then later Pat, a sister of

Phonsine's, took over her team and collected a supportive group to help her, and the project was well launched. Then by slow degrees other groups were formed until there were six teams, and these were responsible for Sunday teams for ten months of the year. Then when these teams were under way, groups from parishes and other groups took over the supplying of the Saturday meals…. When families were involved this usually consisted of three families, one to look after the meat, the second the vegetables and the third the dessert. And each family would bring one or two children.

For most of these volunteers, if not all, it was their first encounter with the poor. Those who lacked nothing (food, clothing, housing, money to spend) met those who had nothing. It was face to face, close up, in the same room, sitting at times at the same table, talking and sharing and laughing. It was in a setting that was like a social, in fact almost a family, occasion. The small-scale work of many hands expanded:

> With the week-end meals taken care of, there then came the idea of getting other groups to take over the giving of meals throughout the week. For on five days of the week we gave meals to twelve of the oldest men who had the greatest need. In time every meal was looked after, but always as an emergency precaution there were always cooked meals in the deep freeze that just had to be thawed out and then heated…. Never once did the men have to go away without a meal.

A new and daring development was that senior high-school students got involved. Through Dr. Peter Pare, who in Dorval was seeing Tony through another bout of pneumonia, Tony met Russ Whalen, the principal of St. Stephen's High School. Russ, who had learned much from teaching in northern Quebec, wanted to convey to his students the essence of Christianity. Slowly, after being well prepared for the initial shock, a few senior students were introduced to "the work." Before long, many of them had organized themselves into teams to work at the House, to visit families and shut-ins, to raise funds by drives to finance medical and dental bills. And, naturally, their own families were drawn in. In time all the high-school grades were active, and in yet more time, more schools, and college students, and the English parishes. At times the House, small as it was, had too many people who wanted to help.

The Labre House paper, *Unity*, in its February 1963 issue, gives a ten-year summary of the House's work. It tells of teams for cooking, serving, cleaning up, and repairing donated clothing. These, for example, now included a teacher and two girls from St. Stephen's High School in Dorval, three to five women from St. Ignatius Parish, two from a roster of 24 from St. Monica's, the Catholic Women's League (CWL) of Dorval, the Christian Family Movement (CFM) of Baie D'Urfé, six girls from Sacred Heart High School, girls from Pius X High School, business women, Bell telephone people, and *Unity* circulation volunteers. The clothing teams, which gave out clothes Tuesdays and Thursdays to some 45 men, included two different Jesuit scholastics each week (who also did chores), and divinity students from McGill University, Franciscan seminarians. Small teams of men took over the House on weekends to give the regulars some time off. Other teams delivered food and furniture and anything needed in the area, a "group of seven" did some fact-finding into the poverty of the area and met every two weeks. By this time, Ray Salmon, who had emphysema, joined as a full-time worker, poverty and all; his efficiency, his bilingualism and his French connections added another dimension to the operation.

Along with this work went the other activities of the House: the Tuesday night talks and discussion, the Thursday Holy Hour at the Little Sisters of Jesus, the House library, the clinic, the poor families directly helped by some richer families, picnics for the old men, the outside talks and panels, the annual retreat, the May pilgrimage to Bonsecours. It was estimated that in 1960, between 400 and 500 people were involved in the work of Labre House. In the 1960s, *Unity* had 3200 subscribers, printing 4,000 copies of each issue. From 1960 to early 1963 it was the only English Catholic paper in the city. And thanks to Bernard Daly, who handled press releases as part of his work with the Public Information office of the Canadian Catholic Conference (CCC) of bishops, that little paper contained news from across the country.

One of the first Labre House retreats was given by Fr. Eric O'Connor, S.J., who along with Charlotte Tansey, Fr. Emmet Carter (later Cardinal of Toronto), Jim Shaw, and others, had just started the Thomas More Institute for Adult Education, a highly creative enterprise and a pioneer in the field. Later, and more than once, the retreat was given by Fr. Dan Berrigan, S.J., who became one of Tony's closest friends.

Mention of Daniel Berrigan, S.J., requires a context: to be a Jesuit at that time still carried with it much of a gloried past. "Jesuit" meant that one could count on disciplined learning and collective wisdom and rationality and saintliness. A Jesuit was one who had been tested during years of formation, whose life was dedicated to the greater glory of God, vowed to obedience, some to special obedience to the pope. People listened to, trusted, accepted what a Jesuit might urge in sermons and retreats and pamphlets and books. Daniel Lord, who died in 1955, was still a recent and revered memory. In Montreal's intellectual world, Eric O'Connor and the Thomas More Institute for Adult Education were already legendary, as were Bernard Lonergan, whose famous *Insight* was just coming out, and Gerald McGuigan, a teacher par excellence, whose contemplative homilies, in later years when he was at St. Ignatius Parish, even ordinary parishioners looked forward to hearing. Jesuits all. *Requiescant in pace.* They and those like them and with them set the tone for the mental – the spiritual and intellectual – world of many Catholics in Montreal. And when Dan Berrigan, S.J., came from Syracuse, New York, to visit the smaller and seedling world of Labre House in the late 50s, he came as himself, of course, but it was as a Jesuit, in all that still glowing context, that he was seen and accepted and deeply appreciated. Whenever possible he gave the Labre House annual retreat. He was always dynamic, energizing, insightful, and passionate about his vision of the poor. Brave in the face of the world's two greatest war machines, the Soviets and the Americans, he protested, always peacefully but provocatively, using his own blood symbolically, burning draft records, also symbolically. In doing so, he violated the taboos of the total state – in fact, broke the law – and was hunted by the FBI and arrested and prosecuted and served his time in prison more than once. Not the first Jesuit to be hunted and jailed. Whether you agree with him or no, he is a prophetic witness.

The Tuesday talks, to take only a few examples, included Gerard Pelletier (on Quebec labour, Asbestos), Claude Ryan (on the lay apostolate), A.G. O'Connor (on Understanding Islam– this in 1953), Fr. Bernard Lonergan, S.J. (on What Use is Philosophy?), and subjects like the Eastern Rite, Judaism, Charles de Foucauld, the liturgy, social work, prisons, current movements in the Church, Abbé Pierre, ecumenism, worker priests, the coming Vatican council. Many from the House were in the Christian Family Movement, others started ecumenical exchanges with people of other denominations (something new at the time), and still others organized help and orientation for foreign students, especially those from Africa. It was a busy time, and it was the 60s.

Most, if not all, of these activities were in some way initiated or suggested or actually started or followed up by Tony. Certainly many of them had to be co-ordinated and orchestrated by him to fit in with the now established routines of Labre House.

He himself remained in the background as much as possible. He wanted to be small-time, anonymous, unnoticed. He avoided publicity; its glare destroyed things. In the late 50s he asked Peter Pare and me not to write about him or keep notes or take pictures or do anything towards compiling a biography. We honoured his request. But he couldn't stay completely hidden: to make "the work" known he had to speak in public. And by all standards, save one, he was a poor speaker.

That one standard is that people listened. He spoke quietly, never raised his voice, never delivered punchlines, never built things up rhetorically, never made points. At times he rambled. He simply spoke, usually without notes, as if he were just joining the conversation. And always it was about "the work," about seen needs, about the circumstances and conditions of the poor of all sorts. It was never about himself, and not about what he personally did, but of what others were doing. He presented a problem not as a problem but as a definite and very real poor person who needed help, and at the same time he gave the solution: another person helping. It became clear, without words, that God's Providence was already there in the form of other persons, those who could help. An audience could easily come to suspect that we were God's Providence to each other. And he did this without quoting Christ's words on the matter. He took all that for granted. This wasn't a tactic, a gimmick, or a conscious technique, not an artifice. It was simply the way he was and what he saw.

The effect on audiences was remarkable. From this quiet, ill-dressed, not-young man, a nobody, came these words about things that had nothing to do with the conventional preoccupations, even religion for that matter, but with the experience of taking the awful risk of trusting Providence. There he stood, wilfully destitute, talking calmly, personifying a condition that would freeze most people with fear: poverty, aloneness, homelessness, illness, the world's contempt. Most people, except the poor. And except those hearers who sensed that here was something quite real and genuine.

He spoke to affluent parishes (to the Holy Name Societies of the period), to students, to religious, to retreatants, to communion breakfasts, to gatherings on special House anniversaries. Sr. Muriel Gallagher, who taught nurses at St. Mary's Hospital in the 1950s, recalls, "I was at a theological conference in Montreal almost by chance, I had heard several priests give some pretty lofty dissertations, and then this little man spoke from his own experience, told about what he was doing, and why he was doing it, and this was Tony Walsh. I was so, just so impressed I guess with the wholeness and the holiness of the man that I really wanted to know more of him, and wanted our students in the school of nursing to come into contact with him." Unknown to him, this characteristic would lead him to another career.

The unrelenting schedule took its toll. He had pneumonia for a third time, had a kidney removed (the result of a sports accident as a young man out West), and had increasing problems with his legs. Ill and tired and worn-and-torn, on May 1, 1966, he brought this second career to an end. If the House were meant to continue, it would. (It does, modified of course, to this day.) But, wisely, he wanted a clean and complete break. He was to be 68 that December.

## A Harvest of Wisdom (1967–1994)

He was free now to rest, and read, to write letters, and visit friends. Living simply was a habit, living in unencumbered poverty still a fact. He knew, of course, from the men he had helped that the old age security, supplement and all, was not enough to live on. It was then $75 a month, with a supplement of $30. Murray Ballantyne persuaded him to accept $25 a month, which he did until pensions improved a few years later. He rented a room "in an ugly area" and went to rest at a small priory in Weston, Vermont. A life of leisure.

But in August 1967, after he had been away from the house about fifteen months, something happened. Colin Maloney, S.J., who as a scholastic had worked at Labre House, was now back from his studies in Rome and had just been made Dean of Studies at Regis College, Toronto, the theologate for the English Jesuit province. He asked Tony to give his theologians a three-day retreat (a triduum). Tony had to think that over. Scholastics he could handle. They were fresh and green novices. But theologians were a different matter; they would have been some ten to twelve years in the Order. He took a month to decide and finally accepted.

There were some 90 students, all close to 30 years old, perhaps a third of them already ordained. Not an uncritical audience. Carefully, Tony began with what the hospital care must have been in Ignatius' day compared to our own, what the French Jesuits did in North America when faced with new languages, modes of travel, ways of living, and finally what challenges they, this class before him, would face in thoroughly secular circumstances where they would be judged first as men, then for competence, and only last, if at all, as priests. The effect he had went beyond the subject or even the words. Here was a man who had had to prove himself, who had actually lived his religion, who was poor in a way they never had been or would be, who spoke from experience, unassailable, irrefutable. A lifetime stood in silent witness. He had done his part.

When the chairman asked for questions, there was silence until one man said he didn't want to talk, but as if he'd seen a good movie, he only wanted to go for a walk and think. The chairman then said anyone was free to do that. "On hearing this, four-fifths of those present fled. Fled was the only word that could describe what happened for they fled in droves." The next day most of them wanted to see Tony personally. Colin asked him to stay three more days, and he did.

In his own un-analytical way Tony describes this new phase: "The Regis College experience had opened up an entirely new avenue of activity. One that continued to grow and with the passing of each year, the following one was even more interesting and enriching." As he saw it, he discovered he was able to do certain things:

> With the passage of time and the meeting and talking with small groups of people, I felt that I should find a word to describe what I was attempting. A certain pattern began to emerge, I would be asked to go to a certain place. If there was funds I would be sent a plane ticket. If there were none, I'd go by bus. At the first gathering everything appeared to be in good order.... But at the second meeting, cracks would appear in the walls, I would then talk to each member in turn, and then give thought as to the core of the problem. And then gradually bring a positive outlook to the situation. Having then formed good communication, I would then clear away the weeds and…then things started to happen…. In the process I found that I had the ability to bring people of like mind and effort together.

He chose "channelling" as an overall term for what he was doing. He didn't see it as anything but the work before him and the fact that he was able to do it. He couldn't see it otherwise. He was not a spectator to himself. People trusted him because he had nothing but his poverty. He played no role, filled no office, had no "job." He wasn't a "professional," he wasn't a "counsellor" paid to hear you out, he had no institution to uphold, governmental or religious, no cause to promote. None of that. He listened to you because it was you who were saying things to him. He was sane, sober, attentive, intelligent, industrious, and (one sensed) holy. He didn't represent anything but a Christian way of life. His CV was his poor past, his recommendations the wretched of our cities, his experience that of a lifetime. Person to person he could give wise personal advice, could assist others in the long process of healing.

He was busy in this third "career," this third phase of his life. In Toronto he assisted some Sisters of St. Joseph in their efforts to live in the poor areas. In time they opened a detox centre for men (Matt Talbot House), which was staffed by trained volunteers; a halfway house for those in recovery; and a sort of home-house for those who worked and would otherwise have to live in a bleak room somewhere. In Puerto Rico, for five winters in a row, he worked with teacher friends and artists on many projects, including one to encourage women to go on to graduate studies. In Kingston, Jamaica, he visited the new Canadian High Commissioner, a friend from army days. Sometime in the early 1970s, an anonymous donor gave him $900 specifically to go to Europe, and he went to Geneva, Vienna (where his parents had been), Rome, and Assisi. For rest and solitude he went once again for a few winters to the Christ in the Desert monastery in New Mexico.

But his past was catching up with him. In 1975 he received an invitation from Fr. Bob Nagy, a chaplain at the Loyola Campus, to accept an honorary Doctor of Laws at the convocation of Concordia

University that June. (In 1978 he received the Christian Culture Award at Assumption University, Windsor; and in 1981 the Ignace Bourget Award given by the diocese of Montreal.) Tony took a month to think it over. He thought he was too much of a nobody to have that honour conferred on him. But he finally agreed to accept it for all those who had been Labre House. At the event, amid all the ceremonial pomp, the presenter, who happened to be this writer, said in part, "He wore donated clothing, he ate donated food, lived in the same run-down district as those who had to, and received the same criticism of not living a constructive life…. Instead of affluence, he chose poverty; instead of conflict, peace; instead of publicity and self-seeking, he chose anonymity; and in an age of fashionable hedonism, he chose a personal celibacy." At the end there was silence for a few moments, and then applause.

About this time, in Montreal, Fr. Joe Cameron let him have a flat at 308 Rielle Street in St. Willibrord's Parish in Verdun. It was on the second floor with a long, steep outdoor staircase and it had lots of cupboard space to handle his accumulating papers. Also about this time, he was faced with a new problem: severe pain in his right ankle, at its worst at night. He didn't let it keep him from his speaking engagements. But at a large seminary his leg gave out as he was being introduced, and he took to using a cane, and then crutches. At the next place, a Jesuit residence, he was given a wheelchair. And when the tour was over, he went to St. Michael's Hospital in Toronto for tests, then to Montreal for another talk, a homily at the Loyola Chapel. Six weeks of tests followed, three months of rehab at the Catherine Booth, and, the leg not yet healed, two weeks in Miami with friends, which helped, and then back to Montreal on his way to a commitment in Newfoundland. As a side trip he was able to visit Dixie MacMaster in Antigonish. In Montreal more recuperation, and soon he was off to England at Raymond Joliffe's (Lord Hylton's) invitation to hold talks about the problems country people were having not far from his estate. This well organized and well prepared trip went quickly and successfully, and he had time to visit Scotland and Ireland before returning to Canada.

In 1976, after an absence of some 30 years, Tony went back to Inkameep for a visit, and on March 24 met in the Okanagan College classroom at Oliver with some 35 people who had known him in his teaching days in the 1930s and early 1940s. A lot of human history. Jean Webber wrote of him and the occasion in "Dr. Anthony Walsh: the Gentle Revolutionary." He would have chuckled at the "Dr. Anthony."

The impact of his quiet talks did not go unnoticed. It was both noticeable and elusive, and impossible to define. He was regularly invited to talk to students, to novices, at retreats, at monasteries. Annually, even twice annually, from the 60s to the 90s, Bill Lawlor (at one time Associate Dean of the Faculty of Education at McGill University) would have Tony talk to his students, an audience of some 40 people. A recurring theme was excellence in teaching and compassion for the learner. His talks had their own unique effect. It seemed to be the mark of the man. It had always been there to see, and now someone decided to do something about it. In 1977 Tony was giving a talk at a retreat at Mary House near St. Joseph's Abbey, a Trappist monastery near Spencer, Massachusetts. Lucien Miller, who taught comparative literature at the University of Massachusetts, at Amherst, was present, and noticed. And thus started a book that would be published ten years later: *Alone for Others.*

He asked Tony to speak and tape his memoirs. "My feeling was that he is at his best when he is spontaneous. I wanted the freshness of the 'talks' I had frequently heard him give in which the Spirit shines through him. Numbers of people attest to this aspect of his speeches in the [taped] interviews which follow [in the book]." There was no need now for anonymity. Labre House was ten years behind him. He would soon be 80. He could look back on his work, in fact his life, and in a period of change and spiritual chaos he could see that his experience might be of help to someone. He had no "system" of spirituality, no "method," he simply practised his religion. His poverty gave him a quite particular freedom.

But Tony didn't speak his memoirs, at least not spontaneously. He typed them out first and then spoke them into the recorder. When Lucien discovered this, they dropped the taping and settled for the manuscripts. Tony was no writer, and the pages, though interesting, are meant as information. They have none of the "spirit" of his talks or his letters, which remains elusive. Lucien's book, however, citing those who knew Tony, from the East and from the West, is a splendid testimonial to that spirit.

Age and ill health were slowly and at times dramatically wearing him down. Friends of all sorts helped him, some with funds, some with services (Pamm Nolan), some with cars (Basil Holland, Art Coveny, Jim Martin), with keeping medical appointments, with days in the country. In the 1980s his godson, Tony Buell, then in his late teens and early twenties, helped him go for walks, and shop, and did personal chores and handyman work for him. In 1987, on a quiet Sunday morning, with Steve Sims, who was then director of Labre House, Tony visited the much changed House. He had been away 20 years. Perhaps it was a farewell. (The next year, with practical foresight, he asked Steve Sims and Jamie Godfrey, a young woodworker, to make him a plain pine coffin. They did, and it was plain, but it was all dovetailed, without screws or nails – a work of art, and love. It stayed in the basement of St. Willibrord's until it was needed.)

In the fall of 1985, he arrived at the Jesuits in Guelph ill with bronchial pneumonia, was hospitalized there, and convalesced, with the added problems of old age, at their novitiate under the care of Fr. Doug McCarthy, S.J., ten seminarians, and a nurse. That November in Montreal his legs got worse, but he managed to go West.

More serious, in early 1988, he had a stroke, followed by a slow recovery until June of that year at the geriatric section of the Royal Victoria Hospital, first to a walker, and finally two canes. Even here, in this new situation, close to 90, he noted and experienced the lot of the old, and was able to encourage some of the nurses and orderlies, harried as they were, to be more humane to their patients.

With all this it became obvious that living at the Rielle Street house was too difficult, and Fr. Joe Cameron advised Tony to apply for residence at the Father Dowd Memorial Home. Once there, he noticed that few residents communicated with each other, and that little was done to help new people with the shock of what was often drastic change: the loss of a spouse, of one's own home, of personal memoried items, a lifetime gone, the dread of what's to come. As usual, he set about doing something about it. He soon found himself on the board of directors. Whenever he could, he spoke to groups or small audiences on the problems of aging. For Tony there was always a "work" to be done.

Since 1978 he had travelled, largely to Victoria, B.C., to escape Montreal's harsh winters. In Victoria, of course, he had other staunch friends and made new ones. He lived in various places – a suite in a private house, an apartment, several times in a motel with kitchen facilities, only once in a place connected with a nursing home. As in Montreal, friends such as the late Harry de Zwager gladly provided transportation. As more and more people learned that he was around, he was invited to give talks to small groups, such as a l'Arche community, Poor Clare nuns, people working with prisoners, people helping others. A helpful friend and organizer, more than a social secretary, was Esther Jedynak, who edited Tony's newsletters – about 35 issues in nine years (1985 to 1993), with a mailing list of close to 150 people. These were a way for Tony to cope with his plentiful correspondence but Esther also used them to explain now and then that funds were low for postage. Poor in money, he was rich in friends.

A man of his intuition and perception was not unaware of the sort of effect he had on people, that "spirit," however indefinable, that others noticed so readily. A clue is provided by a remark he made in 1990 in answering a question for Bill Lawlor's students: "This I can say: that since I left Labre House I have travelled a great deal and met all types of people – there's never a person left me without feeling happier than when they came. What more could I ask of life than that?" This is not a boast, it is more like a discovery.

For his friends, this was a fact that deserved wider recognition. In 1988, Drs. Peter Pare and Peter Macklem began the process of nominating Tony for the Order of Canada. It wasn't difficult to find the many people required to submit the necessary letters of testimony. In April of 1990, in a ceremony at Rideau Hall, accompanied by Peter Pare, he was made a Member of the Order. He remarked in interviews that he was the oldest, 91, and the poorest person ever to become a member. Now he could sign his name Dr. Anthony Walsh, C.M., although he did so only once, in March 1991: "I have always been reluctant to use the word 'doctor' for I got it coming in the back way – unlike others who all but lost blood attaining their degree. There is a great need for dialogue with people of influence. There is the whole health problem very much in the news, especially in Quebec. And though I have only an Honorary Doctorate, I thought it might help." And Esther signed him off as "Tony Walsh, LL.D, C.M."

In his newsletter of March 1991, entitled "The Reality of Aging," his new and last apostolate, he faces things squarely: having to depend on others, dealing with a crabby nurse until she saw things differently, being treated like a child, becoming "a diaper man," having friends die, their valued help (trips to the country) gone, failing eyesight, and having his memory play tricks, though not with Alzheimer's. As Katherine French recalls doing, friends regularly read to him and for him. His observations on his fellow residents at the Father Dowd are acute and insightful. And he found ways of carrying on. "I am now a wheel chair man who uses his heel to steer him around at a much faster pace than I would go with my sturdy white canes or walker." His travelling days were coming to an end.

He looked upon his inevitable death with equal clarity: "My hospital doctor told me that as long as I do not have a fall, I can live a few more years. I have been given time without the pressure of death and have come to the conclusion that I will pass from one type of existence to another but that does not mean that when the time comes I will not suffer. With the time I have left, I will give more thought to others."

That time came, and ended, in 1994. In mid-May he entered the Royal Victoria Hospital in Montreal for the last time. With all his other conditions he was now suffering from low blood pressure, acidosis, and finally septic shock. He was 95, five months into his 96th year. On Saturday, May 28, at about 2:30 in the afternoon, Bill Lawlor, who was at his side, was informed by the nurse that Tony was failing. He left the room to phone Peter and Anne Pare, and while he was thus away the nurse came to tell him that Tony had just died. Surrounded as he was by care, it had happened at a moment when he was alone.

Following his wishes, expressed in his "A Statement," which was regarded as his will, there was no exposure at a funeral parlor. The wake was held at St. Willibrord's church, his body enclosed in his specially ordered and lovingly made pine coffin. The occasion can best be described as seriously joyful. The funeral was held in the same church on Wednesday, June 1. Several people offered reflections, among them Lucien Miller, who read from Dan George; Bishop Neil Willard; Norman Dodge, S.J.; Steve Hagarty; John Carley. Fr. Dan Berrigan, S.J., who could not attend, sent a Zen poem, read by Bob Burns. Monique Jones read the petitions composed by Dr. Thérèse Vanier, Pauline's daughter. And in the congregation,

Tony Buell's daughter Danielle, a little girl of three, slept soundly on the shoulder of Mary Ellen Holland, a lady she had just met. She symbolizes the peace and the reach of Tony Walsh. She could have been his great-granddaughter.

In his will Tony had requested an unmarked grave. That degree of obscurity was too much for his friends, and they had looked about for a way to respect his wishes and at the same time know where he was buried. It seemed impossible. But John Carley, one of those friends, discovered that in the Depression years the then Catholic Welfare Bureau had acquired plots in Notre Dame des Neiges Cemetery for "itinerant Catholic men." There, with the permission of the Foundation of Catholic Community Services, which now has charge of the remaining plots, Tony was buried. It was a fitting compromise: the pauper was still the pauper he had chosen to be. A lot of friends, young and old, were at the graveside ceremony. That year Art Coveny, who had been the Labre House accountant for many years, had a tombstone erected. It was paid for by the few remaining funds that had been Tony's federal old-age pension. It had three lines:

Tony Walsh

1898–1994

Alone for Others

## Epilogue

On December 18, 2002, Andrea Walsh, who is assistant professor of anthropology at the University of Victoria, was in Montreal hoping to visit the present-day Benedict Labre House, to see Tony's grave and to meet with people who had known Tony Walsh in Montreal from the 1950s to his death. As a visual anthropologist, her work in British Columbia with First Nations people had led her to the Inkameep drawings, paintings and other artifacts, which had been saved from a destructive teacher and hidden since the late 1940s by both whites and Indians. Her research also led to the discovery of one Mr. Anthony Walsh and questions about what happened to him after he left Inkameep during the war and the West in 1949. Tony Gray, who had been recently appointed director of Labre House, was able to show her the House, which was being renovated. She found the grave site. And she met with a few people who could tell her about Tony: Connie Dodge; Katherine French; Bill Lawlor; Steve Sims; my wife, Audrey; and me. West met East, and East, West. She had slides of photographs of Tony (in his prime, close to 40) in his classroom at Inkameep, of the artwork of the children, especially that of Francis Baptiste, of the children's acting troupe at the opening of Thunderbird Park in 1941, of them doing their radio broadcast at the CBC in Vancouver. We were enthralled by her presentation, and she by our information about a man she had never seen and was only now learning to call, not "Mr. Walsh," but "Tony."

I bring this up because it says a great deal about Tony Walsh. It shows the depth of his achievement, measured by the effect it had on people, and the persistence over time of his influence. Despite his sometimes comic attempts to remain obscure and unnoticed, the very work he put forward would point to him as its instigator. That "work" was never grandiose, never noisy. He wasn't an activist, he didn't protest anything, didn't rally crowds, or create a movement, or seek followers. He worked quietly, alone for the most part, person to person, and directed people to the "work," which meant, after all, the Christian life. A large part of it was helping others, but it also included doing things well, such as being a competent teacher or a compassionate doctor or a good artist. Whatever it might be, it had nothing to do with making money or acquiring a reputation. All that was secondary. And the "work" created its own effects.

With the children of Inkameep he taught the curriculum well, of course, but he had a broader purpose in mind: to bring out what was there. He saw them as naturally creative (indeed, the image of the Creator), richly nurtured by their culture, and he let them revel in the fact. And this, subtle as it is, stayed with them. This is what spread through the entire community, never to be lost. Interacting with other spirits and trends, it played its part in the formation of committees for the furtherance of Indian crafts, for briefs to the federal government, for proper schools, and changes to the Indian Act, a process that is still going on today.

In 1981 a Committee for the Revival and Furtherance of B.C. Indian Arts reissued *The Tale of the Nativity, as told by the Indian Children of Inkameep*, with the drawings of Sis-hu-lk (Francis Baptiste), which was originally published in 1940. In the new edition Chief Sam Baptiste, the son of the artist, writes a foreword in which he says, "In talking with Mr. Walsh, with some of his former students and with other local people, one feels that during the 1930's the Band lived through some of the happiest and most productive times Inkameep has seen." In correspondence from the late 1930s, researched by Professor Andrea Walsh, Tony Walsh was criticized for "meddling in Indian affairs." It's a good thing he did meddle.

In 1943 in Port Alberni, Tony sensed that there was talent in George Clutesi and knew it had to be drawn out. Jean Webber quotes George Clutesi:

Apparently Tony had heard of my dabbling in the arts. He made many visits to our house before he mentioned or asked if I had any drawings or paintings I would like to show him. For quite some time I was suspicious of this man Tony whom Dr. Rosen seemed to respect very highly. Albeit, I gradually and reluctantly began bringing out paintings I had hidden in closets and old boxes. In due course we found some twenty water colours, and before I knew it Tony had arranged for a local showing in Port Alberni in 1944. This was the beginning of series of one-man shows that went across Canada and as far east as Toronto by 1945.... Had it not been for Tony's untiring counselling and vast store of patience I would never have broken out of the "clamshell" into which I had crawled.

Today, 60 years later, Indian art has become so well known as to be fashionable. Tony Walsh had something to do with that.

Even more obscure was the "work" that became Benedict Labre House. Here there was much less chance of public attention. There were no children to teach, no Legion organization to fit into, no community of "bums" to honour someone who changed things for them. The effects and results here were hidden and not sought out. It is as though he felt that in this work he would never be found out. And so the work, small and local, the little way of the Christian life, went on. And it touched thousands: the constant weekly stream of the destitute, the homeless, the jobless, the alcoholic, the just-out-of-prison, the poor of the neighbourhood, the isolated old, the mentally ill. And it reached and spread among those who did the helping: the volunteers, the teams, the families, parishes, organizations, groups, priests, nuns, teachers, high school and college students, doctors, lawyers, businessmen and, not least, seminarians. It was not planned and programmed; it was not calculated. It just happened. Which is another way of defining Providence.

People speak of his assistance, of his encouragement at a right time in their lives, some of the years of help he gave them. In the late 1970s he mentioned once that in letters to him some people had said they were grateful to Labre House and its newspaper for preparing them for the vast changes in the Church. It is not something that can be measured, or even surveyed. But it is very real, and very present still.

For all that he did and for all the people he dealt with, that "spirit" that Lucien Miller wanted to capture still remains elusive. Those who knew Tony will remember his presence well: he was an average tallish man that most people could meet at eye level. Soft spoken, he would disappear at the first sign of boorishness. He was a great walker. He gave the impression of muscular strength, for work not belligerency. He had a kindly look, a quick twinkle of humour, a ready and easy laugh, a well-made face, not handsome in the bland sense, but marked with character. In repose in profile he looked contemplative, as if his mind were busy, not so much thinking as seeing things calmly. He could get angry, at times, rare times – he had probably seen too much of that as a child to want to add to it himself. He had a quick sense of things, especially people and situations. His account of army life is not primarily a narrative of adventures but rather of experiences and incidents that gave him an insight about the situations he was in and the people making them. He had a knack for sizing things up. His account is more about what he noticed than what he went through. His gift was not for conceptualizing and analyzing but rather for catching on and doing things. It was the knack of being both intuitive and practical.

I believe the shock of his war experience was the turning point of his life. Alone in his personal pain, he was soon to be alone in actuality, and unmarried, and chaste. To get there a strong motivation is needed and an overwhelming experience that casts all else in the background. To begin to understand Tony is to understand what it is to be brought to nothing by shock and suffering, and to be affixed there to dwell and see everything in pain. It is the time of naught, of feeling nothing but the endured aching of one's heart, when even non-existence has a dangerous attraction. In such moments, in such a state, in faith, when being at all is to be alone in this unceasing hurt, one is also alone with God, and so aware. It is then that one begins to see the enormous gift and presence that Christ is. It is then that his words ring, not with rhetoric, but with the fullest reality. Christ, too, had died of his wounds. And this was Mary's to see and hold and weep over. Christ meets the bitterness of our suffering with the mystery of his own suffering. It is virtually impossible to speak of this, much less try to communicate it. It is deep personal unvoiced experience. And with those who have been there, speech is unnecessary. Dixie MacMaster had been there.

In his dealings with others he was a quiet persuader. He was not a "motivator" of the kind who gives pep talks "full of energy." He was not a "psychologizer" of the sort who gives examples of how willful you can get. He was not a self-promoter, not one to set himself up as a success and have you imitate him as the best thing you could do. None of that. He never said, or even intimated, that anyone should do as he did. He was too practical for that sort of sweeping idealism. His example and advice indicated that in the many ways of following Christ a poverty of spirit was a necessary condition. His was a particular vocation which he would impose on no one. His work, as it turned out, was to organize the many people who were willing to do their share.

All this was deliberate, it was a chosen way of life. Its foundations were religious, its motivations rooted in "the spiritual life." That much could be understood. And the "spiritual life" was the life of the Gospels, the life outlined by Christ in the Beatitudes. "Blessed are the poor." What was hard to understand was that here was a man who really wanted to be poor. He wanted, in hard practice, to own nothing. Literally and actually. "Make it your first care to find the kingdom of God, and his approval, and all these things shall be yours without the asking" (Mt 6:33). And owning nothing was not to be a merely passive and negative thing. No, he wanted to do things, many things, and for that he needed a special form of freedom, and that meant relying on God's providence fully. Even at that, he didn't realize how fully that was going to be.

He had to take great care: not to get overwhelmed by the details of running a place like Labre House, by the constant demands, the infinite flow of the poor, the traffic, the unexpected, the sudden, the troublesome. It called for organization on a scale worthy of big-time CEOs. It also called for a self-discipline in orderly living, set times for routine things, all necessary, all creating the context within which this sort of thing could take place. And, above all, it meant he had to have periods of rest, of meditation, of contemplation. Mass, retreats, reading, solitude now and then apart from the aloneness of his position, and the existence of others, however few, who shared his religious outlook. He was not known to have had a spiritual director. If he did, it was the best-kept secret of all.

Many have mentioned his saintliness. And there is no doubt that he was saintly in the sense of being compassionate and kind and generous. He did spend a lifetime helping others. But he was also tough: tough on himself, and tough in the sense of being able to take it, in this case "it" being defeat and suffering and illness and physical infirmities. There was nothing soft or bland about him, no practiced air of smiling fellowship. His gentleness came from disciplined strength, his patience from anger controlled and deflected into a look-for-another-way. No one can read another's heart. But if one uses the Beatitudes as a standard, he was indeed poor in spirit, and poor materially, did in fact mourn, was definitely a peacemaker, was certainly pure of heart, merciful, meek (i.e., patient and obscure), reviled and spoken ill of, though not (mercifully) persecuted. He lived a virtuous life. At times he may have lived it heroically. All this is known by God whom he served, and I am content to leave it at that.

# Bibliography

*A wide range of sources was used in the writing of this book, and many individuals provided information, reminiscences, stories and relevant documents. A list of some of these sources appears below.*

Anson, Peter F. *Abbot Extraordinary: a Memoir of Aelred Carlyle, Monk and Missionary, 1874-1955.* London: The Faith Press, 1958.

Ballantyne, Murray. *All or Nothing.* New York: Sheed & Ward, 1956.

Berrigan, Daniel. *To Dwell in Peace: An Autobiography.* San Francisco: Harper & Row, 1987.

Guest, Dennis. "Old Age Pension," *Canadian Encyclopedia.* Edmonton: Hurtig Publishers, 1985.

Hart, Liddell B.H. *History of the First World War.* London: Pan Books Ltd, 1973.

Merriman, Brigid O'Shea, O.S.F. *Searching for Christ: The Spirituality of Dorothy Day.* Notre Dame: University of Notre Dame Press, 1994.

Miller, Lucien. *Alone for Others: The Life of Tony Walsh.* Toronto: Community Concern Associates Ltd, 1987.

Miller, Wiliam D. *Dorothy Day: A Biography.* San Francisco: Harper & Row, 1982.

*The Tale of the Nativity: as told by the Indian Children of Inkameep.* British Columbia: 1981. With a Foreword by Chief Sam Baptiste and illustrations by his father, Sis-hu-lk (Francis Baptiste), from the edition of 1940.

Walsh, Andrea N. "Drawing on Identity: The Inkameep Day School," in *Untold Stories of British Columbia: Papers presented at the conference 'Untold Stories of British Columbia' 1-2 March 2002.* Victoria: Humanities Center, University of Victoria, 2003.

## Web Sites

Walsh, Anthony. Untitled Document, "The Inkameep Indian School," n.d., on website: www4.vipnet/osoyoosmuseum/inkameep_walsh.html

Webber, Jean. "Dr. Anthony Walsh: the Gentle Revolutionary," 1976, on website: www4.vip.net/osoyoosmuseum/walsh76.html

## Thesis

Nolan, Patricia A.E. "Benedict Labre House: 1952–1966: the History of an Unofficial Lay Apostolate." M.A. Thesis, Concordia University, Montreal, 2001.

## Newspaper Articles

Blazina, Randy. "Art teacher helped natives gain equal rights." *Osoyoos [B.C.] Times,* 20 March 2002, p. 19.

Chamberlain, Adrian. "Native prodigies that time forgot." *Times Colonist (Victoria),* 1 March 2002, sec. C.

Johnson, Wendy. "Lost Okanagan artwork resurfaces." *Oliver [B.C.] Chronicle,* 17 April 2002, p. 11; "Inkameep art collection priceless." 29 May 2002, pp. 1, 2; "Inkameep Day School art work will be showcased in Vancouver." 18 September 2002, p. 10.

*Unity* (Montreal). February 1961, April 1961, February 1962, May–June 1966.

## Newsletters

Walsh, Tony. Newsletter (untitled) 1985–1993, ed. Esther Jedynak. Copies supplied by Esther Jedynak and George Cook.

## Interviews Cited

French, Katherine. 9 December 2003.

McAsey (Branswell), Mary. 17 July 2002, Phone Interview.

Tansey, Charlotte. 17 July 2002, Phone Interview.

## Tapes

Meggs, Peter. Interview with Tony Walsh, "Open Door," CBC Radio, Fall 1990. Supplied by George Cook.

Walsh, Tony. Address to students, Faculty of Education, McGill University, 13 February 1990, 30 March 1978. Supplied by Bill Lawlor. Talks and interviews in Victoria, B.C., supplied by Esther Jedynak.

## Archives

Hagarty, Stephen, depository for Lucien Miller's materials in researching and preparing *Alone for Others*. Contains Tony Walsh's "Memoirs," originals and edited MSS, transcripts of taped interviews with people who knew TW, letters, some copies of the paper *Unity*, and so on. Titling is repeated from originals to edited versions, with variations, and is not consistent, pagination is local to each chapter, sheets are unbound, MSS are not in any fixed order but must be organized.

Martin, James, miscellaneous and discontinuous papers left by Tony Walsh, unclassified and unnumbered and unpaginated; letters and papers by James Martin.

*Note:*     Tony Walsh's papers are now housed at the Department of Anthropology, University of Victoria Archives, British Columbia.

**AGMV** Marquis

MEMBER OF SCABRINI MEDIA

Quebec, Canada
2004